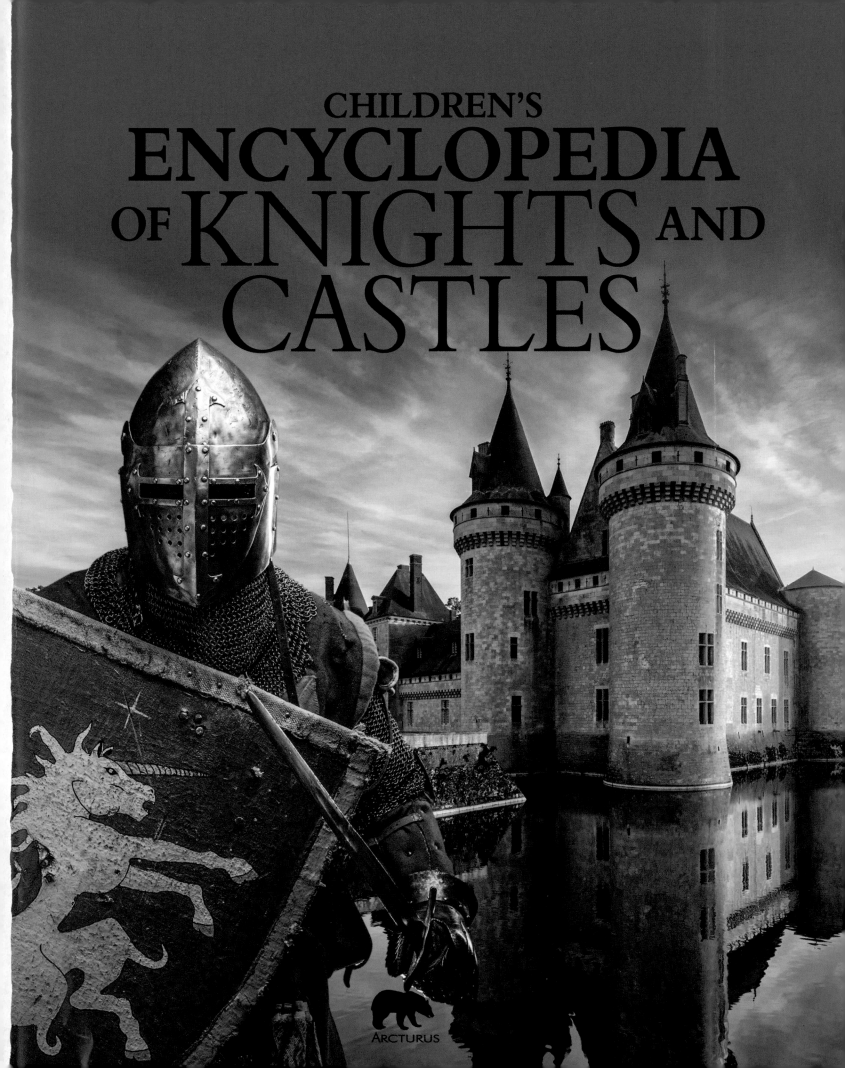

CHILDREN'S
ENCYCLOPEDIA
OF KNIGHTS AND
CASTLES

Arcturus

Picture Credits

Every attempt has been made to clear copyright. Should there be any inadvertent omission, please apply to the publisher for rectification. Interiors: Akg-images, Vienna Austrian National Library 39; The Art Archive 23, /Aarhus Kunstmuseum Aarhus Denmark/Dagli Orti 4, /Ciano d'Enza Emilia Romagna Italy/Dagli Orti 6, /JFB 14, /Biblioteca Nazionale Marciana Venice/Dagli Orti (A) 17, /Museo del Baregello Florence/Dagli Orti 19, /Musee des Arts Decoratifs Paris/Dagli Orti (A) 20, /Jarrold Publishing 25, /University Library Heidelberg/Dagli Orti (A) 27; The Art Archive 53, The Art Archive/Museo Storico Topografico Firenze com'era Florence/Dagli Orti 32, /British Library 34, 67 /Dagli Orti 35, / Museo Civico Bologna/Dagli Orti 36, /Bibliotheque Municipale Rouen/Dagli Orti 38, /Museo Civico Citta di Castello/Dagli Orti 17, /University Library Prague/Dagli Orti 42, /Museo d'Arte Nazionale d'Abruzzo L'Aquila/Dagli Orti 44, /Issogne Castle Val'Aosta/Dagli Orti (A) 45, / Real biblioteca de lo Escorial/ Dagli Orti 63, /British Library 47, 64, /Musee Conde Chantilly/Dagli Orti 65; The Art Archive/Bibliothèque Nationale Paris/HarperCollins Publishers 68, /British Library 74 (Ms Add 42130, f.202v), /Burgerbibliothek Bern/Eileen Tweedy 93, /John Meek 92, /National Gallery London/Eileen Tweedy 84, /Reading Museum/Eileen Tweedy 70; The Art Archive/Biblioteca Nazionale Marciana Venice/Dagli Orti (A) 100, /Bibliothèque Nationale Paris 112, 113, /Bibliothèque Nationale Paris/Dagli Orti (A) 106, /Bibliothèque Nationale Paris/HarperCollins Publishers 110, 120, /Bodleian Library Oxford 118 (Auct D inf. 2 11 folio 44v), /British Library 115, /College of Arms/John Webb 102, /Musée Condé Chantilly/Dagli Orti 107, /Musée des Beaux Arts Orleans/Dagli Orti (A) 105, /Musée de la Tapisserie Bayeux/Dagli Orti 97, 122 /University Library Heidelberg/Dagli Orti 101,/Victoria and Albert Museum London/Eileen Tweedy 103; Bridgeman Art Library/British Museum London 96, /Birmingham Museums and Art Gallery 121, /Sheffield Galleries and Museums Trust 98; Bridgeman Art Library/Guildhall Library, Corporation of London, UK 40, / Bridgeman Art Library/Bildarchiv Steffens 55, /Giraudon 48, 51, /Archives Charmet 66; British Library 116 (MS 42130 f82), 119/British Library 76, 94 (Ms Harley 4431. f.135), 86; English Heritage/HIP 13; National Archives 10; Pierpont Morgan Library, New York 78 (Ms 638, f.27v), 82 (Ms 775, f.122v); Royal Armouries 69, 72, 94 (Inv. No. II 334), 75, 85, 89, 95 (Inv. No. II.3, VI.379), 108; Science and Society Museum Picture Library 54; Zul Mukhida 49; Topham Picturepoint 5, 29/© 2001 Topham Picturepoint 56, / © Brian Yarvin/The Image Works © 2003/ Topham Image Works 57, University Library Prague/Dagli Orti 59/Dagli Orti 60; Trinity College, Cambridge 80 (Ms 0.9.34 f.24r). All other images from Shutterstock. All cover photos from Shutterstock.

ARCTURUS

This edition published in 2021 by Arcturus Publishing Limited
26/27 Bickels Yard, 151–153 Bermondsey Street,
London SE1 3HA

Authors: Sean Sheehan, Kathy Elgin, Saviour Pirotta, Fiona Macdonald, Patricia Levy, and Christopher Gravett
Editors: Lisa Regan and Susie Rae
Designers: Chris Halls, Mind's Eye Design Ltd, Lewes and Trudi Webb
Illustrators: Peter Dennis and Adam Hook
Managing Editor: Joe Harris
Design Manager: Jessica Holliland

ISBN: 978-1-3988-0942-0
CH008651US
Supplier 29, Date 0621, Print run 11398

Printed in China

Castles and the Medieval World

Troubled Times

This account, written by a monk in England in 1137, describes the troubled times that accompanied the building of castles:

"Every great man built himself a castle and held it against the king; and they filled the whole land with these castles. They cruelly oppressed the wretched men of the land with castle works. When the castles were made, they filled them with devils and evil men. Then they took those men who they imagined had any property, both by night and by day, peasant men and women, and put them in prison for their gold and silver, and tortured them with unutterable tortures."

(From *Castles in Medieval Society*)

Castles first appeared in northern Europe in the tenth century, in a period of time known as the early medieval age. Before the medieval period, the Roman empire had provided stability for much of Europe, with its good roads, trained armies, forts, and defensive walls. Beginning in the fifth century, however, the empire began to break up, and everything began to change. There were large migrations of people across Europe, from the east and from the far north. Vikings, from Norway, Sweden, and Denmark, settled in northern France and became known as Normans (the "Northmen"). There was also a dramatic expansion of Islam, and a Muslim empire developed across parts of the Mediterranean world. A king named Charlemagne, or Charles the Great, ruled much of western Europe, but after he died in 814, his empire broke up.

This is a modern painting of Rolf Gangr, leader of Viking pirates, on the coast of northern France at the start of the tenth century.

Contents

By around 1000, most of western Europe had settled into a number of different kingdoms. These states were based around ruling families who saw their kingdoms as their own private property. The rulers wanted to protect their property and have soldiers ready and willing to fight for them. At the same time, they wanted a secure home in which to live and enjoy their wealth. This was the medieval world out of which castles first appeared and developed.

The history of the Normans explains why castles came to be built in England. In 1066, the Normans invaded England, and after defeating the ruling king, they set about controlling their new kingdom. They needed to show their authority and crush rebellions that broke out across the country. In 1070, there was a general uprising in the north of England, as well as smaller ones in the south of the country. Danish ships arrived to support the rebels. It was this kind of military insecurity that made the Normans build castles.

Castles were fortified country houses, and they were built throughout the medieval age from the tenth to the fifteenth centuries. Wherever they were built, from northern Europe to the Middle East, they shared certain features that were common to most castles.

The thirteenth-century castle Burg Gutenfels stands above the Rhine River overlooking Pfalzgrafenstein, a fortress built in 1326.

Medieval Life
Only a tiny minority of people—the very rich—could afford to build and live in a castle. Most people spent their lives in the countryside, working on a small farm for which they paid rent and taxes, and living off the land. Towns were just beginning to develop in the early medieval age. Most people could not read or write. A peasant farmer was unlikely to live beyond the age of 30, and the average height of a man was 5.4 feet; women were a little shorter.

The Parts of a Castle

Dungeon

Dungeon

A castle keep was originally called a "donjon," an old French word. When the Normans first came to England, they brought a ready-made wooden donjon for their king. It was set up in Hastings, where the Norman king defeated the English ruler. Over time, the word "donjon" came to mean the room in the tower where prisoners were kept. Later, the word "dungeon" came to mean "prison," and because the donjon moved to below ground level in a castle, it came to mean an underground prison.

The central part of a castle was its tower, also called a keep, usually round or square in shape. The number of levels within the keep would depend on its size and the wealth of its owner, but one floor would make up the castle's main hall. The hall was the heart of life in a castle. People would gather here to eat and be entertained. Other levels and rooms within the keep would be used for bedrooms, and although a separate kitchen would later be added, food was cooked outdoors to avoid the risk of fire in castles made of wood. In an emergency, the keep was a castle's last line of defense: This is where people could lock themselves in and hold out against

The ruins of a real tenth-century castle in Italy bear little resemblance to our romantic image of medieval castles.

The main parts of a castle are the keep, walls, bailey, gatehouse, and a moat.

an enemy for as long as possible. Usually, the castle well would be below the keep, so that there was always a source of water in the event of a siege.

A strong wall, now called a curtain wall, was built around the outside of the keep. At first, it was made of wood, but later stone was used. The enclosed area between the inside of the wall and the keep was known as the bailey. As an open space, the bailey provided room for soldiers to gather, and since soldiers needed horses for transportation, the bailey also provided space for stables. Other outbuildings for storing equipment and supplies could also be built. Larger castles could have an additional second wall built around the original one; this created two baileys, an outer and an inner one.

The gatehouse was a castle's front door, and since it was the place where an enemy might try to break in, it needed to be especially well protected. It helped to dig a moat—a trench filled with water or kept dry and sometimes planted with sharp stakes—around the outside of the walls. The gatehouse would face the only bridge over the water. By attaching the bridge to the gatehouse and making it possible to draw it up or down, the resulting drawbridge formed a strong defense against enemies.

A Castle Keep
This is a description of a large castle keep, or central tower. It was written in 1117 and refers to a wooden castle built around 75 years earlier: "The first floor was on the surface of the ground, where were cellars and granaries, and great boxes, tuns [containers], casks [barrels], and other domestic utensils. In the level above were the dwelling and common living room of the residents, in which were the larders [food storage], the rooms of the bakers and butlers, and the great chamber in which the lord and his lady slept."
(From *The Medieval Castle*, Philip Warner)

Types of Castles

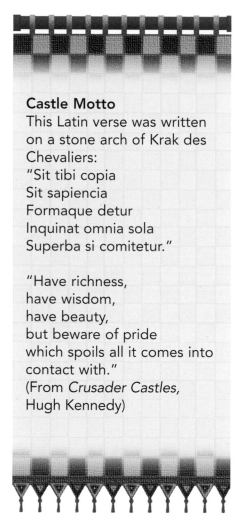
The earliest type of castle was built on a large mound of earth that could be as high as a six-floor house. Digging out earth for the mound created a ditch that could form the castle moat. A wall of earth and timber formed a defensive barrier around the keep. The central mound was called a "motte" in French, from which the word "moat" comes, and this type of castle came to be known as the motte and bailey castle.

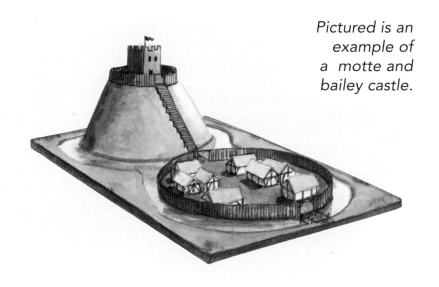

Pictured is an example of a motte and bailey castle.

At the end of the eleventh century, stone began to be used instead of wood and earth for both the keep and the castle walls. Around the same time, the first of six Crusades got under way. The Crusades set out to expel Muslims from land in the Middle East regarded as sacred to Christians. Crusaders voyaged through what is now Turkey and the Middle East and they saw a new style of stone fortifications. They were on a far grander and more impressive scale than anything seen in Europe. There were long defensive walls, with towers sticking out from them at regular intervals, from which defenders could overlook an attacking force and prepare for their arrival.

The fortified walls of Muslim castles and towns were also built to include areas of bare rock, even cliff edges, making such a castle far more difficult to attack. As the Crusaders set about building their own castles in the Middle East, they were influenced by these Muslim designs.

Crusader castles led to the building of larger and more ambitious castles back in Europe. Massive gatehouses were constructed, and towers were added to castle walls. This new type of structure came to be called the concentric castle, because there was more than one surrounding wall. By the thirteenth century, when concentric castles were becoming common, some were being built without a keep. Instead, inside the outer wall, there was another wall connecting a series of towers. Even if an enemy broke through the outer wall, there was, in effect, a second castle securely defended and stored with provisions.

The Crusades also taught European rulers the military value of building more than one castle in a particular territory. With a group of castles, the soldiers inside them could then support one another. Any enemy that wanted to try to gain control and ownership of a territory would have to take on the combined force of a group of castles.

Krak des Chevaliers
The finest and most elaborate Crusader castle, Krak des Chevaliers, was first built in the Middle East in what is now Syria, in the second half of the twelfth century. It could hold up to 2,000 people and had two very strong stone walls surrounding it. The Muslim military leader, Saladin, decided in 1188 that it was too powerful to be captured. The walls and projecting towers were fitted with slits for archers to fire from and positioned in such a way as to cover most of the outside ground.

Krak des Chevaliers in Syria is the greatest Crusader castle.

Building a Castle

The most important person in the building of a castle was the master mason. Partly an architect and partly an engineer, he would discuss building plans with the person who wanted a castle built. A building contract would often be drawn up between them, setting out the costs and what the builder was expected to do in return for the money being spent. The contract would be written twice on a single sheet of parchment, and then the sheet was cut along an indented line. Each party to the contract kept their own copy, which matched the other exactly, including the course of the wavy or zigzag line along which they had been cut. This kind of contract was known as an indenture.

After agreeing on the kind of castle to be built, the master mason used a basic knowledge of geometry to figure out the shape and proportions of the planned building. A quarry was needed as close to the building site as possible, where square

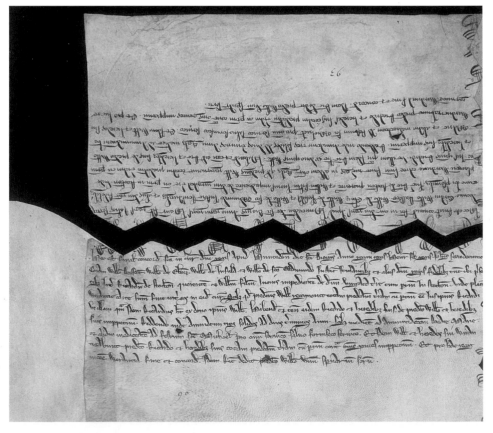

This is an example of an indenture, clearly showing the zigzag line.

Pictured is a master mason supervizing work on a stone block for a castle keep. The keep can be seen in the background.

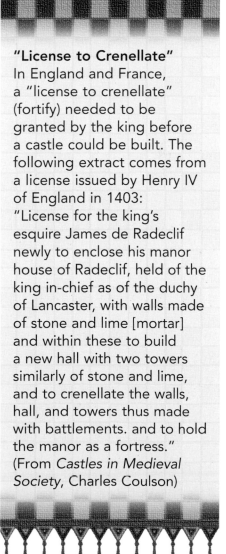

"License to Crenellate"
In England and France, a "license to crenellate" (fortify) needed to be granted by the king before a castle could be built. The following extract comes from a license issued by Henry IV of England in 1403:
"License for the king's esquire James de Radeclif newly to enclose his manor house of Radeclif, held of the king in-chief as of the duchy of Lancaster, with walls made of stone and lime [mortar] and within these to build a new hall with two towers similarly of stone and lime, and to crenellate the walls, hall, and towers thus made with battlements. and to hold the manor as a fortress."
(From *Castles in Medieval Society*, Charles Coulson)

blocks of stone could be cut out of the ground. Axes and chisels of various sizes were used to cut the stone, and finer chisels and mallets were used to carve decorative designs onto cut stones. Mortar, which was needed to hold the stone together, was made by burning chalk or limestone in ovens specially prepared for the purpose. The burning produced quicklime, to which water and sand were added to make the mortar.

Carpenters, metalworkers, and other masons all worked under the master mason. A smith was also needed to replace and sharpen the various building tools. Ladders, scaffolding, ramps, and pulley systems were all used in the building of a castle. Walls were mostly filled with rubble and mortar, then finished with a quality stone called ashlar, which had been cut to size and smoothed carefully. In northern Europe, the building of a castle only took place during the warmer months of the year. At the end of summer, walls were covered over to protect them from winter rains and frosts, and work would start again in the springtime. A large castle could take years to complete.

Keeping Out the Enemy

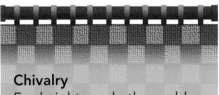

Chivalry

For knights and other nobles, war was seen as something brave and heroic. Both sides in a war shared similar ideas about winning glory and showing charity and loyalty. This heroic code of conduct was called chivalry, although it did not extend to the treatment of Muslims and Jews. Such non-Christians were usually regarded as inferior, people who did not deserve the normal rules of conduct. Knights, if they were defeated by their own kind, could expect to be ransomed rather than killed. Common soldiers, however, were expected to fight and die for their lords. Chivalry protected knights and nobles from the grim realities of war.

A castle was built to withstand attack from an enemy. Any attack would have to cross the moat and break through the walls or the gatehouse to enter the castle. In order to strengthen the gatehouse area, strong towers known as barbicans were added. They would usually be part of the gatehouse wall but projected forward, so as to provide extra cover for defenders.

Soldiers defend a castle from being attacked.

Warkworth Castle, in northern England, shows arrow loops and battlements.

In order to strengthen castle walls against the effect of battering rams, stonework was added to the bottom of walls. This made them thicker and gave them an outward slope. Large stones, dropped from above on the castle walls, could bounce off the slope and into the bodies and faces of enemy soldiers. Castle walls, especially above the gatehouse, had overhangs with holes built into them. Known as machicolation, castle defenders could then more easily drop stones or boiling oil onto the attacking soldiers.

Castle walls were also built with narrow openings known as arrow loops, from which a defender could shoot through. From the inside, the walls at the sides of the arrow loop opened widely, so a bowman could stand comfortably. From the outside, however, narrow arrow loops were difficult to shoot at. The top of a castle wall had openings about 2.6 feet wide called crenels, and the sections of wall in between were called merlons. These crenels and the much wider merlons (both up to about 6 to 10 feet in height) formed a castle's battlements. From the battlements, bowmen could fire their arrows at an advancing enemy.

The inner side of battlements were usually left exposed to the castle interior, with a narrow walkway that was only wide enough to hold a few men. If an enemy did manage to climb the walls and clamber over the battlements, he was exposed to attack from inside the castle.

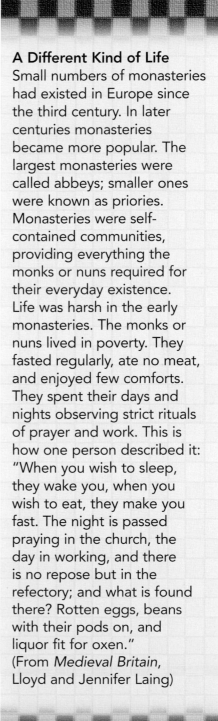

A Different Kind of Life
Small numbers of monasteries had existed in Europe since the third century. In later centuries monasteries became more popular. The largest monasteries were called abbeys; smaller ones were known as priories. Monasteries were self-contained communities, providing everything the monks or nuns required for their everyday existence. Life was harsh in the early monasteries. The monks or nuns lived in poverty. They fasted regularly, ate no meat, and enjoyed few comforts. They spent their days and nights observing strict rituals of prayer and work. This is how one person described it: "When you wish to sleep, they wake you, when you wish to eat, they make you fast. The night is passed praying in the church, the day in working, and there is no repose but in the refectory; and what is found there? Rotten eggs, beans with their pods on, and liquor fit for oxen." (From *Medieval Britain*, Lloyd and Jennifer Laing)

Castle Under Siege

Food for a Siege

A castle's ability to withstand a long siege depended on its supply of food and water, and a good supply of grain was essential if flour was to be available for making bread over a long period of time. Krak des Chevaliers, a Crusader castle, had ovens, huge jars for storing oil, hundreds of sacks of grain, and a windmill on one of its towers for making flour from the grain. With reliable wells to supply water, as well as large cisterns for collecting rainwater, a castle could withstand a siege for many months.

A siege was an attack on a castle that was prepared to defend itself. The enemy force would try to break through the castle walls using a variety of means. The stone walls, more difficult to set on fire than the wooden walls of earlier castles, could sometimes be mined from underground. This was not possible if the walls were built on a foundation of natural rock or if the water in the moat could not be drained elsewhere. Soldiers could try to climb the walls with ladders or break through with a battering ram. Both sides fired arrows and stones with bows and slings, and by the twelfth century, the crossbow was being used. There were also various types of siege engines that could launch stones weighing up to 550 pounds, and occasionally dead horses or rats would be hurled into a castle in the hopes of spreading disease. Movable towers built of wood could be wheeled up to castle walls, but defenders were sometimes ready for this. They dug concealed pits whose covering would give way and unbalance a tower when it moved forward. If an attacking force could not break though the walls, they

An early form of cannon is used to attack this castle.

Siege machines are used here to attack a castle that is well-protected with machicolations.

could always camp outside and wait patiently until the castle was starved into surrendering. Supplies and reinforcements were prevented from reaching the castle, and the defenders would have to try and manage on whatever supplies of food and arrows they already had. Injured soldiers needed to be treated, and infectious diseases such as dysentery were likely to spread in the cramped conditions of a castle under siege. At the same time, however, the attacking army also needed to be accommodated and fed, and this put pressure on its ability to maintain a long siege.

Mining a Castle

This account of the siege of a Crusader castle by Muslims in 1115 describes the mining of a castle:

"As soon as they got to the tower, they enlarged the tunnel in the wall of the tower, supported it on timbers, and began to carry out, a little at a time, the bits of stone produced by boring … They then began to cut dry wood and stuff the tunnel with it. Early the next morning, they set it on fire. We had just at that time put on our arms and marched under a great shower of stones and arrows to the trench, in order to attack the castle as soon as the tower tumbled over. As soon as the fire began to have its effect, the layers of mortar between the stones of the wall began to fall. Then, a crack was made. The crack became wider and wider, and the tower fell."

(From *Crusader Castles*, Hugh Kennedy)

Feudalism and Castles

I n medieval Europe, a king or emperor held the most power in a country, but one person could not single-handedly control all of his territory. He needed the support of other wealthy and influential people, known as barons, whom he could trust and rely on for the supply of soldiers in the event of a war. Land would be given by a king to loyal barons, and these nobles, having received permission from the king, could build their own castles.

This diagram shows the class structure of medieval society.

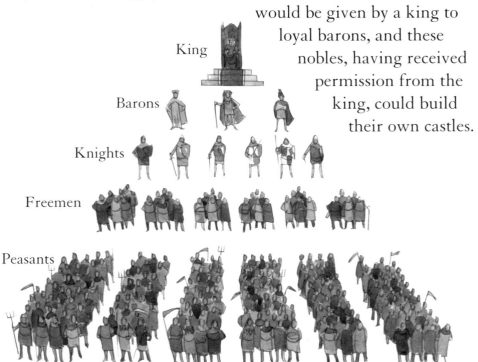

King

Barons

Knights

Freemen

Peasants

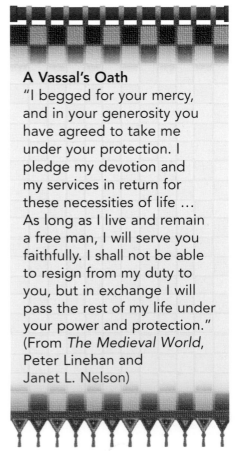

A Vassal's Oath
"I begged for your mercy, and in your generosity you have agreed to take me under your protection. I pledge my devotion and my services in return for these necessities of life … As long as I live and remain a free man, I will serve you faithfully. I shall not be able to resign from my duty to you, but in exchange I will pass the rest of my life under your power and protection."
(From *The Medieval World*, Peter Linehan and Janet L. Nelson)

Knights were a special class of soldiers who were obliged to serve their king or baron in times of war. In the early medieval period, knights often lived in the castles of nobles and formed the garrison—this was the body of soldiers ready to fight and defend the castle. Over time, many knights became wealthy lords, especially as a result of the Crusades, and were no longer obliged to fight. Instead, knights could now pay money to their king or baron. This system, known as scutage, allowed many knights to live on their own land. As a result, a castle's garrison often came to be made up of soldiers and less wealthy knights who hired themselves out to lords.

The relationship between kings, barons, and lords was an important part of the medieval system. It was based on the exchange of land in return for service, which usually included military service. The vassal, the person providing service, swore loyalty to his ruler and offered his services in return for the land he was given. This became a ceremonial occasion known as homage, which took place in the chapel of a castle or in a cathedral.

Peasants lived on and farmed the land that belonged to the nobles. The peasants had few rights and, after handing over a percentage of the produce they grew to the nobility, had barely enough to keep themselves alive. Their work allowed the nobles to enjoy privileged lives in their castles. In return, the peasants were allowed to live on sections of the land. Serfs were a class of peasants who were the most poorly treated. They were little better than slaves and could be bought or sold like a piece of property.

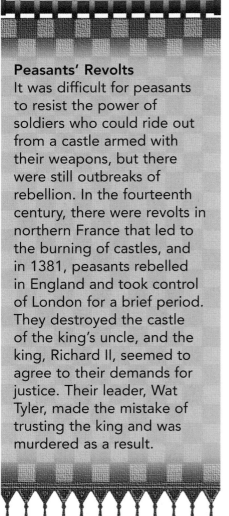

Peasants' Revolts
It was difficult for peasants to resist the power of soldiers who could ride out from a castle armed with their weapons, but there were still outbreaks of rebellion. In the fourteenth century, there were revolts in northern France that led to the burning of castles, and in 1381, peasants rebelled in England and took control of London for a brief period. They destroyed the castle of the king's uncle, and the king, Richard II, seemed to agree to their demands for justice. Their leader, Wat Tyler, made the mistake of trusting the king and was murdered as a result.

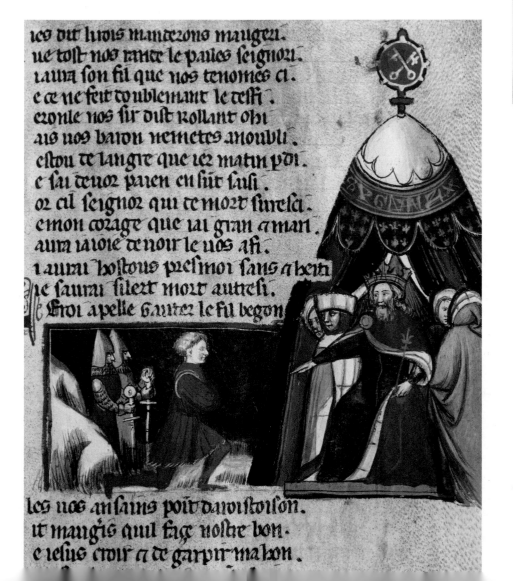

This fourteenth-century illustration shows a homage ceremony or perhaps a king in the act of making someone a knight.

17

Living in a Castle

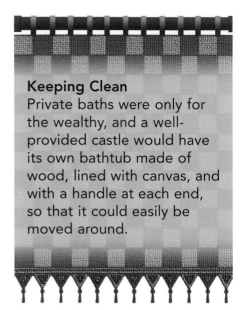

Keeping Clean
Private baths were only for the wealthy, and a well-provided castle would have its own bathtub made of wood, lined with canvas, and with a handle at each end, so that it could easily be moved around.

Castles, all of which were privately owned, were far more than military buildings. Although a king or high-ranking baron would spend most of his time touring around the country, many castles were homes where a lord and his family lived and passed most of their time. Naturally, they would try to make their home as comfortable and attractive as possible. The inside and outside of castles were painted brightly, and care was taken in their upkeep. Henry III of England ordered the rainwater spouts on the Tower of London to be lengthened, so that watermarks would not stain the fresh-painted, gleaming white walls.

An artist's impression depcts various activities inside a medieval castle.

The hall in an early medieval castle would only have a hole in the roof for smoke to escape from, and there was little ventilation. Herbs might be scattered over the floor and on the straw used as mattresses, to sweeten the air inside the castle.

The fireplace and tallow candles were the main source of light. As the medieval age progressed, improvements were made to the living style of castle residents. The use of stone made it possible to build fireplaces into the wall and to add chimneys. The original keep of an old castle was often inadequate for living quarters, and new rooms could be built, sometimes surrounding a central courtyard. The basic division between the hall with its fireplace and a chamber for sleeping could be extended into groups of rooms, depending on the wealth of the castle owner.

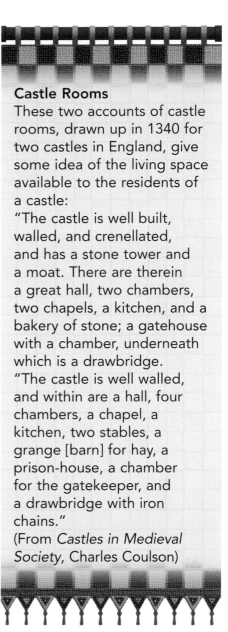

Castle Rooms
These two accounts of castle rooms, drawn up in 1340 for two castles in England, give some idea of the living space available to the residents of a castle:
"The castle is well built, walled, and crenellated, and has a stone tower and a moat. There are therein a great hall, two chambers, two chapels, a kitchen, and a bakery of stone; a gatehouse with a chamber, underneath which is a drawbridge.
"The castle is well walled, and within are a hall, four chambers, a chapel, a kitchen, two stables, a grange [barn] for hay, a prison-house, a chamber for the gatekeeper, and a drawbridge with iron chains."
(From *Castles in Medieval Society*, Charles Coulson)

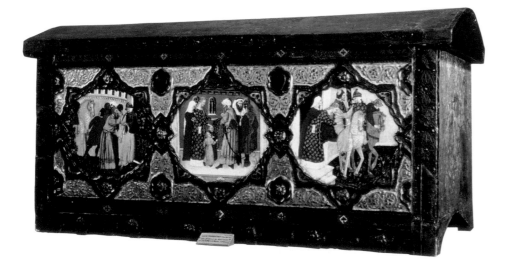

Furniture was a luxury in the medieval age, even for the wealthy few who lived in their own castle. There were beds, but chairs were uncommon, and an average-size castle would possess very few. The most important person at any meeting always had the use of a chair—this is the origin of the term "chairperson." The basic item of furniture was a chest, where clothes and valuables, such as metal tableware, could be stored. Nobles who moved around the country and stayed in their different castles took their chests with them.

This wooden chest of a nobleman from the early fifteenth century is decorated with scenes from the Crusades.

Working in a Castle

Paying Wages
The following accounts are for Chirk Castle in Wales at the end of the thirteenth century, and they refer to the wages bill for one year. A shilling (s) was made up of 12 pennies (d).
"And in wages of the porter of the Castle for the same time 60s 10d taken by the day 2d.
And in wages of one park-keeper for the same time 30s 5d taken by the day 1d.
And in salary of one Chaplain for celebrating in the Castle for the year 53s 4d."
(*From* The Medieval Castle, *Philip Warner*)

Depending on its size, a castle was a home to a number of people. If the castle owner was a king or an important baron that owned lots of land and homes, much time was spent moving from one castle to another. An official called a castellan, or constable, was appointed to be in charge of the castle when the king or baron was absent. Other barons and lords lived full time in their castles, along with their wives and children, with various attendants and workers to service their needs.

In times of peace, a castle's garrison might consist of only a few soldiers, but knights and more soldiers could always be called upon when necessary. When touring from one castle to another, a king or baron needed bodyguards, and servants were essential to attend to their needs while staying in a castle.

This painting showing ladies-in-waiting performing their work in a medieval setting.

A garrison made a castle like a police station, but other people working in a castle made it seem more like a town hall. Officials called sheriffs could use a castle as their base, collecting payments from peasants and applying laws. Records needed to be kept, and clerks who could read and write were required for this purpose. The clergy were among the few who were literate, and clerks were often church officials who worked under the chaplain, the priest in charge of a castle's chapel.

Here is an artist's impression of an armorer at work in a castle.

Servants and a blacksmith were needed to tend the horses, and an armorer carried out repairs to weapons and armor. Carpenters were needed for a variety of jobs, from making a soup bowl to a bed. There were cooks and servants called trenchermen who carried and served food at the table. Ladies-in-waiting lived in a castle as the personal attendants of a noble family. There were also laundresses, bakers, and brewers of beer.

Food and the Kitchen

Producing food was a vital matter in the medieval age because it was not something that could be taken for granted. Indeed, the power and influence of those who built castles partly depended on their ability to provide food for their knights, attendants, and servants. The very title "lord" comes from an Old English word "hláford," which meant the keeper of bread.

Grain, usually made into bread, was the basis of the medieval diet, although the kind of bread eaten depended on a person's place in the feudal order. Wastrel, white bread from grain that was finely sieved and ground, was reserved for a lord and his family; poorer people ate brown bread made from bran or rye. Bread, left to grow hard for a few days after baking, also made disposable plates that were called trenchers. Forks were

Kitchen staff are busy preparing and cooking food in a castle.

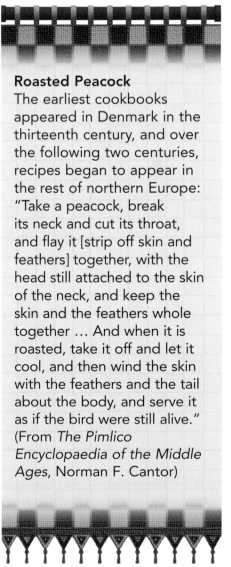

Roasted Peacock
The earliest cookbooks appeared in Denmark in the thirteenth century, and over the following two centuries, recipes began to appear in the rest of northern Europe: "Take a peacock, break its neck and cut its throat, and flay it [strip off skin and feathers] together, with the head still attached to the skin of the neck, and keep the skin and the feathers whole together ... And when it is roasted, take it off and let it cool, and then wind the skin with the feathers and the tail about the body, and serve it as if the bird were still alive." (From *The Pimlico Encyclopaedia of the Middle Ages*, Norman F. Cantor)

not used, and food was eaten by hand or with spoons after it had been cut up with a knife. People carried their own knives, which were kept in special cases or carried in a sheath. The drinking of wine was reserved for the wealthy, while ordinary people consumed beer or a drink called mead, made by fermenting honey and water.

The nobility in a castle ate far better food than that available to peasants working in the fields. Poor people could not afford to eat meat on a regular basis, but beef, mutton, and a variety of wild birds provided meat dishes for lords and their families. The kitchen, a vital part of any castle, was kept separate from the main hall, but later it came to be connected by a passageway. A kitchen might use an open fire, or an oven could be set into a wall. A large castle would have a separate bakery for the daily production of fresh bread, as well as a pantry for storing food. Kitchen equipment, such as a cooking pot, was made of iron, copper, or bronze, while pitchers for holding wine and other liquids were made of pottery.

Castle Luxuries

Head coverings and hats were popular in the medieval age, and the nobility displayed the more fashionable styles.

The medieval age covered many centuries, and over time, there were improvements in the nature of castle life. In the tenth century, there was little commercial trade between the different areas of Europe. By the fourteenth century, trade links across Europe and the Mediterranean were well established. The benefits of this trade were available, not to the majority of people who farmed the land, but to wealthy families who lived in castles. The nobility were able to purchase goods and luxuries that were previously difficult to obtain.

The rich owners of castles displayed their wealth in the clothes they wore, using materials such as silk, satin, and mink. Damask,

a rich silk fabric woven with elaborate designs and often in a variety of shades, got its name from the city of Damascus in the Middle East. The Crusades had opened up to Europeans a whole range of luxury goods, including tapestries, carpets, and spices, as well as fine silk fabrics. From Russia came a variety of furs that were used to line clothes and bed covers, providing extra warmth in the cold and drafty rooms of a castle. In France and Holland, a plant called madder was used to dye cloth into beautiful hues from orange and red to purple, helping to distinguish the owner of such clothes. The growing of flax made linen clothing more important, and shirts and underwear began to be worn.

The Fur Trade
Peasants in Russia and Finland captured and skinned minks, otters, foxes, squirrels, beavers, martens, stoats, bears, and other animals. The skins ended up in markets in eastern Europe, and from there, they were sold on to other merchants in western Europe. The final stage was making garments from the furs. These were then sold to wealthy people who could afford them. The more pelts, or animal skins, that went into a piece of clothing, the higher the social status of the wearer. A full fur coat worn by a French king was said to come from over 350 pelts.

Patterned carpets and embroidered fabrics on chairs were luxury items available to the wealthy owners of castles.

As castles became bigger, extra rooms were added, and chambers could be provided for guests. Tapestries were hung from walls that acted as screens dividing bedrooms, and ceilings might be painted with a design or a picture. The greatest wealth of a castle was likely to be in the chapel, in the form of vestments that used expensive materials, as well as plates and church ornaments made from precious metals like gold and silver.

Entertainment and Leisure

A castle was a home, and when military matters could be put to one side, it was a place where people enjoyed themselves when not at work. Children played games similar to today's leapfrog, blindman's buff, and tug-of-war. A variety of ball games were played by young people, but although they resembled games such as tennis and hockey, rubber had not been discovered yet, so balls did not bounce.

In the medieval age, there were professional entertainers who would visit a castle to play music and sing ballads. Music was popular and it was danced to, as well as played as an accompaniment to storytelling. Minstrels, troubadours, and jongleurs were names for different types of entertainers who sang and played musical instruments. Feasts were an important

In the thirteenth century, jousts became a popular form of entertainment. Blunted weapons were frequently used to avoid serious injuries.

A fourteenth-century German manuscript shows Emperor Otto IV playing chess with a woman.

part of medieval social life, and musicians would be hired for a castle banquet that celebrated an official event or holiday occasion.

The importance of war in medieval life meant that it affected forms of entertainment and leisure. Part of the popularity of the game of chess in medieval times was due to its military character—"checkmate" derives from the Arabic "shah mat," meaning "the king is dead"—and, in the course of time, the terms "castle," "castling," and "knight" were added to the language of the game. Tournaments and jousts, where mounted and armed knights engaged each other on horseback, were a combination of entertainment, sport, and military training.

For peasants, hunting was a practical activity intended to produce a meal on the table, but for the nobility, hunting for wild game and birds combined sport with military training. It allowed lords and knights to try their skills using various weapons, and castles would often be close to a forested area that was the private property of the castle owner. In this way, part of a castle estate became a private game park for the rich to hunt boars and stags. Falcons and hawks were also trained to seize smaller birds, and this sport became known as falconry. A special building in a castle, a mew, was used to keep a falcon.

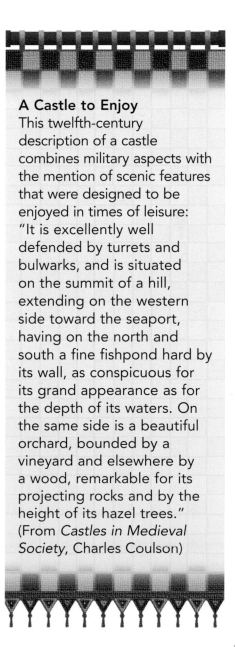

A Castle to Enjoy
This twelfth-century description of a castle combines military aspects with the mention of scenic features that were designed to be enjoyed in times of leisure: "It is excellently well defended by turrets and bulwarks, and is situated on the summit of a hill, extending on the western side toward the seaport, having on the north and south a fine fishpond hard by its wall, as conspicuous for its grand appearance as for the depth of its waters. On the same side is a beautiful orchard, bounded by a vineyard and elsewhere by a wood, remarkable for its projecting rocks and by the height of its hazel trees." (From *Castles in Medieval Society*, Charles Coulson)

Castle Fatigue

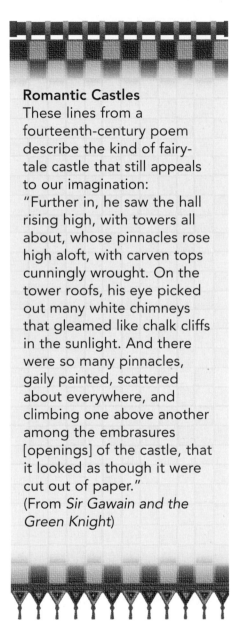

Romantic Castles
These lines from a fourteenth-century poem describe the kind of fairy-tale castle that still appeals to our imagination:
"Further in, he saw the hall rising high, with towers all about, whose pinnacles rose high aloft, with carven tops cunningly wrought. On the tower roofs, his eye picked out many white chimneys that gleamed like chalk cliffs in the sunlight. And there were so many pinnacles, gaily painted, scattered about everywhere, and climbing one above another among the embrasures [openings] of the castle, that it looked as though it were cut out of paper."
(From *Sir Gawain and the Green Knight*)

The first cannons were simple, often ineffective devices. But by the late fifteenth century, improvements had turned them into important weapons for attacking castles.

Before the use of gunpowder, most means of attacking a castle relied on the muscle power of soldiers. Gunpowder changed this because it released energy that could drive heavy objects, such as cannonballs, against a target. It could do serious damage without relying on the physical strength of large numbers of men.

Another important technological development toward the end of the medieval age was the ability to melt iron ore in a blast furnace. The liquid iron was poured into molds of a particular size and shape, and in this way, iron cannons could be manufactured. By using the explosive power of gunpowder, cannons could direct and smash balls of cut stone against the walls of a castle. By delivering a force greater than any previous engine of war, gunpowder and cannons indicated the end of the age of castle building.

The new technology, however, was also available to the defenders of a castle, and castle building did not suddenly come to an end. Early cannons were difficult to use and not very mobile, and handheld cannon guns were used by soldiers defending castles. Gunports for the new weapons were cut low into the walls, so as to aim them directly at an attacking force. Arrow and crossbow loops were adjusted to handle hand cannons, and vents were added to carry away the smoke caused by the exploding gunpowder.

Gunpowder and the cannon, however, meant that castles could be successfully attacked without having to resort to long and costly sieges. In 1453, Turkish forces broke through the mighty fortifications of Constantinople using cannon guns to good effect. By the sixteenth century, castles were of military importance in only a few parts of Europe—Austria, for example, which was under threat from the advancing Turks. Castles in other areas were being converted into military forts and barracks, or they were turned into grand homes. The idea of a castle as a fortified house that needed to be defended against a possible attack was becoming an idea of the past. The medieval age was over.

Fairy-Tale Castles

Centuries after the medieval age, castles began to be built once more. This time, however, they were built as romantic reminders of a past age. They were fairy-tale castles like the castle of Neuschwanstein, built in Germany toward the end of the nineteenth century, which inspired the Walt Disney logo. Another example, Castle Coch in Wales, was built using the plans of a thirteenth-century castle that once stood on the same site. Medieval castles still appeal to us, and people visit restored and rebuilt castles across Europe and in parts of the Middle East.

Castle Coch, built around the same time as Neuschwanstein Castle (see panel, above), is a far more realistic example of what a medieval castle actually looked like.

Timeline

476   The last Roman emperor loses power to tribes invading western Europe.

711–1250   Years in which most of Spain is held by Muslim rulers.

814   The death of Charlemagne, a king whose empire included large parts of the Roman Empire.

1066   Norman forces invade England, and castles are built to secure their authority.

1070   A rebellion in the north of England against Norman authority.

1095–9   The First Crusade, a successful one that included the capture of Jerusalem.

1147–9   The Second Crusade, a failure.

1142–1271   Krak des Chevaliers (below), a very strong castle in the Middle East, is held by Crusaders.

1188   Saladin, leader of the Muslims, gives up an attempt to capture the Crusader castle, Krak des Chevaliers.

1189–92   The Third Crusade, with victories for both Christian and Muslim armies.

1202–4	The Fourth Crusade, a failure.
1220	From around this time, glass windows are made for castles.
1250	Castles with more than one stone wall—concentric castles—begin to be built.
1320	The first cannon is produced in Europe.
1326	The first picture of a cannon appears in England.
1350	Cannons are used regularly in castle sieges.
1381	The Peasants' Revolt in England.
1400	Smiths begin mixing the ingredients of gunpowder in water to produce a fine powder that is easier to use than earlier forms of gunpowder.
1453	Turkish forces successfully attack the strong fortifications of Constantinople using cannons.
1500	Most castles no longer function as fortified homes, except in some parts of Europe under threat from Muslim forces.
1869	Building work starts on Neuschwanstein Castle in Germany, in the style of a medieval castle (right).
1875	Castle Coch in Wales is built in a medieval style.

Life Outside the Castle Walls

Letter from King John of England to families who want to live in his new town, Liverpool, 1207:

"The king to all who wish to have burgages [rental houses and shops] in the town of Liverpool, greetings. Know that we have granted to all who take up burgages at Liverpool that they shall have all the liberties [rights] and free customs [freedom to trade] as enjoyed by any other free borough on the seacoast in our land. And so we command that you travel there safely and in our peace, in order to receive your burgages and to live there."

Life inside the castle was separate from life outside the walls, but there was plenty of interaction between the two. In times of peace, castle residents would venture outside for trade, and possibly for their health and to visit friends or family. Some trades and skills were best learned in the nearby towns or cities and then put to use within the castle.

A medieval town was a special place, separate from the countryside. Often, it was shut away from its surroundings behind strong gates and walls. People living in medieval towns had special, different jobs—making things to sell, working in shops or offices, or providing food and drink, lodgings, or entertainment. These trades made medieval towns rich, interesting, and exciting. But they were also noisy, dirty, dangerous, and sometimes deadly places to live.

This is the rich trading city of Florence, Italy, circa 1490. Many fine churches, bridges, merchant houses, workshops, and family homes are crowded inside its strong, protective walls.

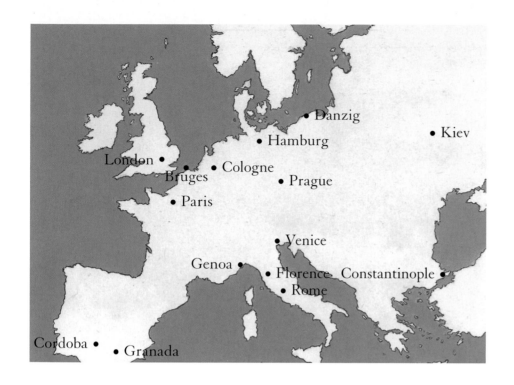

The map shows important towns of medieval Europe.

There were towns all over Europe, from northern Scandinavia to the southern shores of the Black Sea. They all had very different histories. Some, like Marseilles in France, Constantinople (Istanbul), now in Turkey, and York in England, had survived from ancient Greek and Roman times. Others, such as Winchester, in southern England, had been built as safe strongholds during the warlike years that followed the collapse of Roman power around 450 CE.

Some towns, such as Aachen, in southern Germany, or Rheims in northern France, grew up between 500 and 1000 CE, close to government headquarters or an important royal church, and shared in their prestige. But many of the richest towns, for example, Hedeby in Denmark, Dublin in Ireland, Bruges in Belgium, and London and Norwich in England, developed as trading places. They were close to safe ports, beside busy long-distance tracks, or at river crossings.

Many European towns were founded before 1000 CE. But in the next three centuries, thousands of new towns—over 125 in England alone—were deliberately created by powerful people such as bishops or kings. By founding them, they hoped to make money from renting town property and from collecting taxes on town trade. Some new towns were sited next to lords' castles for protection, such as Edinburgh in Scotland.

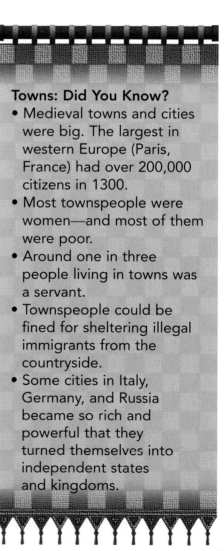

Towns: Did You Know?
- Medieval towns and cities were big. The largest in western Europe (Paris, France) had over 200,000 citizens in 1300.
- Most townspeople were women—and most of them were poor.
- Around one in three people living in towns was a servant.
- Townspeople could be fined for sheltering illegal immigrants from the countryside.
- Some cities in Italy, Germany, and Russia became so rich and powerful that they turned themselves into independent states and kingdoms.

Who Lived in the Towns?

Town Freedom

Medieval people had a saying: "Town air makes you free." An unfree peasant who ran away from a lord's estate and lived in a town for a year and a day could claim freedom forever. He could also apply to become a burgess—if he managed to earn enough money to pay the joining fee and had friends among the existing burgesses to support his claim. Many poor people could not afford to become burgesses, so over the years, town communities became divided. A small, elite group of burgess families owned town property and ran town governments. Most other citizens were simply workers.

Historians estimate that about 20 percent—one in five—of the European population lived and worked in towns. Some people were born there to long-established town families. Others took the decision to migrate to towns and make a new life, away from the countryside.

Unlike today, men and women who wanted to live in a nearby town could not just simply move there and be allowed to play a full part in town life right away. Town dwellers —often called "burgesses" or "citizens"—had special rights and privileges, which they guarded jealously. For example, only they could own or rent houses and shops in a town, store their goods in its warehouses, or tie up their cargo ships there. Or they might be free from heavy taxes charged on goods brought by outsiders into town to sell.

Europe's first banks began business in towns. These late fourteenth-century illustrations show moneylenders, borrowers, and bankers.

In return for these rights, burgesses also had special duties—for example, not to shelter thieves and cheats, and not to give away the town's trading secrets. They also had to share the task of running the town's local government or choosing officials, such as a mayor and bailiffs, to do this for them. Only men could be full burgesses. Women shared in their husband's or father's rank—and wealth—but could not own town property or take part in town government.

Throughout the Middle Ages, towns grew in size as people migrated to live in them. People came for different reasons. Some were optimistic: They came to look for work or to learn a new skill. They wanted to be free (see panel on page 34), and they hoped to make money. Some were professionals, such as priests, teachers, doctors, lawyers, and scribes, who set up schools, offices, and consulting rooms in many towns.

But many people who came to live in towns were driven by desperation, not hope. They included farmworkers who had lost their land, homeless families, abandoned wives, poor widows, orphaned children, and injured soldiers. If they could not find work in the country or get help from their friends and families, their only hope was to make their way to a town. There, they might survive by doing odd jobs or receiving charity.

Oath sworn by new burgesses of Ipswich, eastern England, circa 1450:
"Hear this, you bailiffs, coroners, and portmen [town officials] and all other men present, that I shall henceforth be a true burgess and keep secret the counsels and private matters of the town and its Great Courts, and not discuss them. Nor shall I disguise the goods of any man as my own goods, so that the town shall not lose any right or profit ... And I shall also be obedient to present or future bailiffs ... And I shall also pay my fair share of taxes ... And I shall support and maintain the town ... with my body, goods, and chattels ... so help me God."

Local councils built grand meeting halls to display their town's wealth and pride. This town hall in Prague, Czech Republic, was built in the late fourteenth century.

Markets and Fairs

Trade was the most important activity in almost every town. In the early Middle Ages, most trade took place at markets and fairs. These were held regularly—markets once or twice a week, fairs on holy days once or twice a year.

Customers try on garments and buy fabric at the cloth market in Bologna, Italy, around 1450.

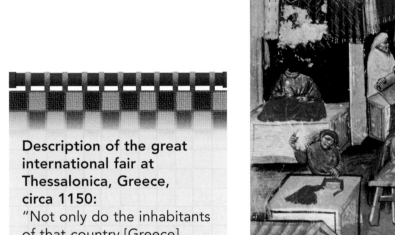

Description of the great international fair at Thessalonica, Greece, circa 1150:

"Not only do the inhabitants of that country [Greece] flock to it in great numbers, but multitudes also come from every race, including Russians ... Italians ... Spaniards, Portuguese, and French. What I saw there was a number of merchants' booths, set up in rows opposite each other ... there was every kind of material woven or spun by men or women ... plus goods from nearby Greece and Macedonia, goods carried by ship from Italy, Spain, and Egypt, and Asian goods brought from Constinople on horses and mules."

Markets sold everyday foods, such as fish and meat, butter, cheese and eggs, fresh fruit, vegetables, and herbs. Market stalls also sold useful items, such as rough clothing, heavy leather shoes, farm tools, pottery, wooden bowls, and combs made of cow horn. Hungry customers could also buy fresh bread and beer made by brewers and bakers in towns—and hot meat "coffyns" (pies), a popular take-out snack.

Men and women walked or rode many miles into towns to bring goods to sell at markets or to buy items they could not grow or make for themselves. Most villages had no shops, and markets also gave buyers the chance to see goods produced in different places throughout their local area. An ordinary villager could not possibly visit them all.

Medieval people looked forward to fairs as special occasions where they could buy exotic goods, such as perfumes or spices, and meet traders from different lands. Unlike markets, which closed at the end of each day, a fair might last for a week or more. Roaming entertainers, musicians, sports games, dancing, and even special religious processions all added to the fun.

The importance of trade was reflected in the layout of most European towns. At their heart, most had a large marketplace for trader stalls. In wealthy towns, there might also be a covered market, sheltered by a wide roof, or a grand trading hall, where merchants could display valuable goods in comfort and safety. The marketplace would also have a cross or a saint's statue (to protect customers and traders) and an office for market officials. They checked weights and measures and kept a lookout for counterfeit coins.

Fairgrounds were usually sited on the outskirts of a town, so merchants would have plenty of space to set up their booths. Nearby, there would be grassland where they could park their carts and wagons, pitch their tents, and graze their horses.

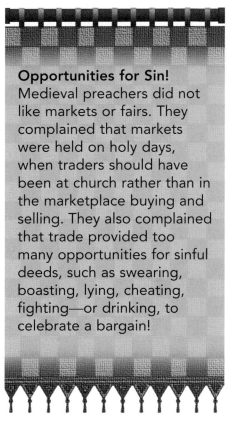

Opportunities for Sin!
Medieval preachers did not like markets or fairs. They complained that markets were held on holy days, when traders should have been at church rather than in the marketplace buying and selling. They also complained that trade provided too many opportunities for sinful deeds, such as swearing, boasting, lying, cheating, fighting—or drinking, to celebrate a bargain!

Market traders displayed goods made in family workshops—like these leather pitchers and shoes— on wooden stalls in open-air market places. Cloth awnings sheltered traders and customers from rain and sun.

Crafts, Trades, and Industries

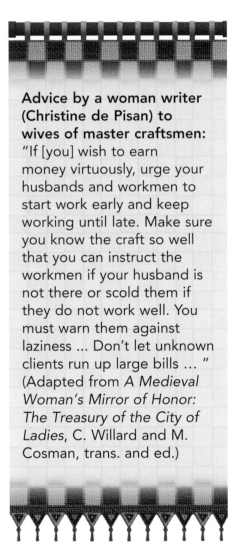
As well as being busy ports and crowded trading places, towns were also where people made things. They had no big factories like our modern cities, where goods are mass-produced by machine. Instead, craftsmen and women worked at home or in small workshops and studios, where they made all kinds of useful items by hand.

For example, they hammered pewter to make pitchers and dishes, melted wax and tallow to make candles, carved wooden furniture, knitted socks, designed hats and caps, wove twigs into baskets, mixed cosmetics and medicines, shaped delicate gold trinkets, or stitched fine embroidery. Craftwork was slow and painstaking, and so craft goods could be expensive. Compared with today, most medieval people owned very few possessions, but they treasured them—usually for life.

Expensive luxuries are for sale at an (indoor) market in France around 1450.

A fourteenth-century tailor measures a customer before making a new robe. His apprentices (trainees, see page 41) sit sewing clothes carefully for other customers by hand.

Many town houses had a back room or a yard where family members and their servants worked. But some trades, such as blacksmithing, pottery, or glassmaking, needed special equipment, including dangerous fires and furnaces. They were limited to certain streets of the town, where a careful watch could be kept to make sure that they did not set nearby buildings on fire.

Other trades, especially tanning leather or dyeing cloth, were so smelly (both used stale urine in their work—it provided essential chemicals) that they were banned from the town itself. Almost always, tanners and dyers had to work outside the city walls.

Raw materials for all these industries had to be carried to workers and workshops. They came either from ships in town ports or from the countryside nearby. Haulage was big business in medieval times. Vast quantities of heavy, bulky goods—such as wood and stone used for building—had to be transported to towns on lumbering carts pulled by horses, oxen, or mules.

Similar carts were used to carry barrels of wine, salted meat, sticky honey, or dried beans and peas from country farms to city shops, as well as sacks of freshly ground flour from windmills and water mills to bakers in busy towns. Huge bales of raw wool and heavy hanks of spun thread had to be delivered to spinners and weavers, along with bulky bundles of feathers for mattress makers. Haulers also had to handle more troublesome living cargoes, such as the 50,000 sheep and 20,000 goats taken for sale to just one city (Florence in Italy) every year.

High Status Trades
All craftworkers were skilled, but some enjoyed higher social status than others. They made luxury objects for rich clients using costly materials. These were the top trades in Paris, France, around 1400:
- goldsmiths
- embroiderers
- makers of fine armor
- tapestry weavers.

Going to Work

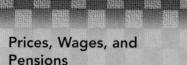

Prices, Wages, and Pensions

Craft guilds tried to control prices charged by their members and wages paid to them. They also laid down rules for working hours. In London, for example, no guild member was supposed to work for longer than 16 hours a day in summer or 12 hours in winter. Guilds collected fees from members to pay for meeting halls, feasts, church services, and to help fellow workers. For example, it cost 3s 4d (about two weeks' wages) to join the carpenters' guild in London in the mid-fourteenth century. The same guild paid a pension of 2d per day to sick members—about two-thirds of a normal day's wages.

Town trade—and all town craft manufacturing—was controlled by groups called "guilds." There were two different kinds: merchant guilds and craft guilds.

Merchant guilds were groups of rich, powerful traders who worked with town governments to control trade in towns. They fixed the prices at which goods could be sold in their town's market, checked weights and measures, tried to keep members from cheating customers or failing to pay their debts, and did all they could to increase the fame and prosperity of their town.

Craft guilds were brotherhoods of skilled workers who joined together to maintain high craft standards, improve working conditions, and care for members (and their families) who were old or sick. They also provided training in each of the craft's special skills.

This is the coat of arms (official badge) of a medieval guild—the Salters Company of London, England.

A master stonemason watches while an apprentice refines his stonecutting skills.

Training started at about 12 years old, when parents paid for a boy to become an apprentice. For the next two to seven years, he lived and worked with a master craftsman's family, learning all he could. He received food, clothes, and lodging, but no pay. At the end of his apprenticeship, he could join the craft guild as a "journeyman" (worker paid by the day). If he liked, he could leave the family who trained him and seek work elsewhere. Finally, when he felt really confident about his skills, he could show a piece of his best work to senior members of the guild. If they approved this "masterpiece," he became a master craftsman. He could set up his own workshop, employ journeymen, and train apprentices of his own.

Girls could be apprenticed as well as boys. They usually trained at crafts like embroidery or tailoring, where many women were employed. Some women, such as Mabel of St. Edmunds in England, who made a robe for King Henry III around 1240, were highly praised—but they could not belong to any guilds. Full guild membership was for men only, although wives could be joint members with their husbands if they worked in the same family firm. A widow could also continue her husband's business as if she were a guild member, but this was a special privilege. To help one another, some expert women workers in Paris (France) and Cologne (Germany) formed their own craft guilds, though these were never as powerful as the men's guilds.

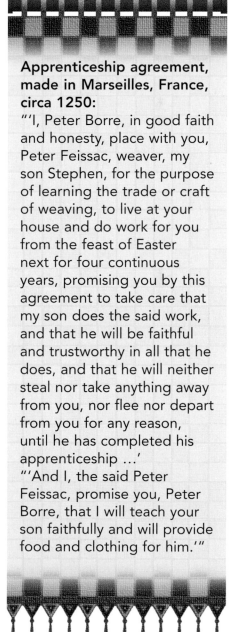

Apprenticeship agreement, made in Marseilles, France, circa 1250:
"'I, Peter Borre, in good faith and honesty, place with you, Peter Feissac, weaver, my son Stephen, for the purpose of learning the trade or craft of weaving, to live at your house and do work for you from the feast of Easter next for four continuous years, promising you by this agreement to take care that my son does the said work, and that he will be faithful and trustworthy in all that he does, and that he will neither steal nor take anything away from you, nor flee nor depart from you for any reason, until he has completed his apprenticeship …'
"'And I, the said Peter Feissac, promise you, Peter Borre, that I will teach your son faithfully and will provide food and clothing for him.'"

Food and Drink

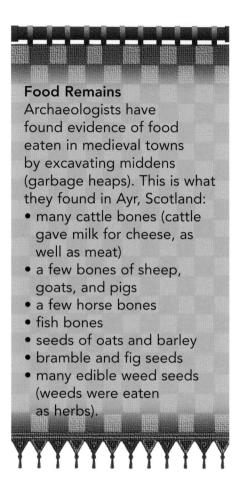

Food Remains
Archaeologists have found evidence of food eaten in medieval towns by excavating middens (garbage heaps). This is what they found in Ayr, Scotland:
- many cattle bones (cattle gave milk for cheese, as well as meat)
- a few bones of sheep, goats, and pigs
- a few horse bones
- fish bones
- seeds of oats and barley
- bramble and fig seeds
- many edible weed seeds (weeds were eaten as herbs).

Unlike castle grounds, town houses had no space for keeping animals, except perhaps a horse in a stable, or a pig shut up in a small backyard sty. And there were few gardens, orchards, or fields inside town walls. So, town dwellers had to rely on meat, fish, grain, fruit, and vegetables—and also olive oil, butter, cheese, and wine—produced by workers in the countryside or around the coast.

What people ate depended on how rich or poor they were. Rich families consumed large quantities of meat, which was often served in spicy sweet-and-sour sauces. They also liked white wheat bread—a medieval status symbol, sweet wine, and sugary treats, such as marzipan (almond paste).

In polite society, food was served in dishes called "messes" that were shared between two or four diners. People helped themselves from the "messe" with spoons or knives—forks were not yet widely used. As the meal began, each diner was given a thick slice of stale brown bread called a trencher. They used this as a disposable plate to hold their food, and as they ate, fat and sauce soaked into it.

Customers wait to buy fish at a busy Italian shop, around 1400.

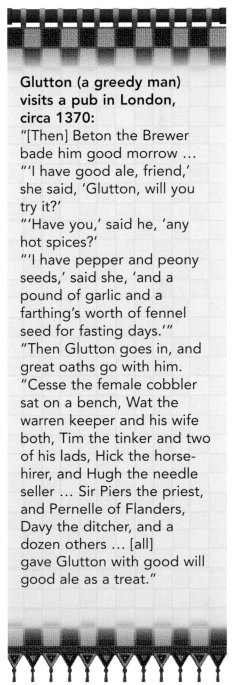

As well as cooking food for their families over open fires, townswomen brewed ale—the main medieval drink—from barley, water, and yeast.

Ordinary workers ate large amounts of coarse wholewheat bread; workers consumed 5.5 pounds per day or more! They also ate oatcakes, barley bannocks (a type of biscuit), porridge, vegetable soup, peas, lentils, bacon (the cheapest meat), eggs, and whatever fruit and vegetables they could find. Men, women, and children mostly drank weak ale—this was sugary and starchy and provided extra nourishment. Because ale was boiled during the brewing process, it was also safer than water to drink. To add interest to their plain-tasting meals, ordinary families liked strong seasonings, such as pepper, garlic, and onions. The rich complained that working people stank of them!

Shopping, cooking, and serving meals was women's work. (So was cleaning houses, washing clothes, caring for husbands and children, and entertaining visitors.) Wealthy women had servants to do all these tasks; women married to ordinary citizens, such as shopkeepers or journeymen, had to help with their husbands' businesses as well.

Providing food could also be a way for women to earn money. They brewed ale, ran public houses (pubs), or cooked meals and let rooms for lodgers. Some women ran their own businesses as food sellers. They made luxury foods, such as fruit syrups and sweetmeats (candied fruit), to sell to rich customers, or they bought perishable goods such as milk from country producers and resold them at higher prices in towns.

Glutton (a greedy man) visits a pub in London, circa 1370:
"[Then] Beton the Brewer bade him good morrow …
"'I have good ale, friend,' she said, 'Glutton, will you try it?'
"'Have you,' said he, 'any hot spices?'
"'I have pepper and peony seeds,' said she, 'and a pound of garlic and a farthing's worth of fennel seed for fasting days.'"
"Then Glutton goes in, and great oaths go with him.
"Cesse the female cobbler sat on a bench, Wat the warren keeper and his wife both, Tim the tinker and two of his lads, Hick the horse-hirer, and Hugh the needle seller … Sir Piers the priest, and Pernelle of Flanders, Davy the ditcher, and a dozen others … [all] gave Glutton with good will good ale as a treat."

Health and Welfare

Medieval towns were not very healthy places to live. Many only managed to survive because new settlers constantly arrived. They replaced existing citizens, who died more quickly and at a younger age than if they had been living in the countryside. Medieval people knew that they were taking a chance when they moved to a town, but they probably believed it was worthwhile. They either hoped to grow rich or wanted to escape from a miserable existence in the country.

There were beggars in all medieval towns. Many of them were sick or had disabilities. They could not find work and relied on charity to survive.

An Italian pharmacist mixes medicine around 1450. Jars of herbs, spices, and chemicals can be seen on the shelves.

What killed townspeople? Mostly, dirt and disease. Town water was often polluted, and in homes without lavatories, people threw human waste into the gutter or out of upstairs windows into the street below. Horses and donkeys, used to pull carts, also created waste, which was often just piled up in the open air. Town businesses, such as butcher shops, produced rotting garbage that was a breeding ground for bacteria, rats, and flies.

In medieval times, people did not understand how bacteria caused dangerous illnesses such as dysentery or typhoid, which led to sickness and diarrhoea and killed many young children. (Around four out of every 10 medieval babies did not survive to reach five years old.) They also did not know how rats, flies, and fleas passed on sickness. Rat fleas were especially dangerous. In 1348–50, their bites (which injected bacteria into the blood) spread an epidemic of a killer disease called the plague. Overall, about one-third of the people in Europe died, the majority of them town dwellers.

Homelessness, cold, and hunger were also serious problems in many medieval towns. Poor people usually slept in their employer's house—on the floor of the workshop, for example, or in a drafty attic. Out-of-work families found lodgings where they could. Sometimes, they rented a single room in a run-down larger building. But often, they had to make do with temporary shelters in storage sheds, or they slept rough on the streets.

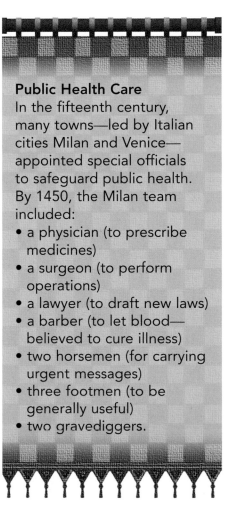

Public Health Care
In the fifteenth century, many towns—led by Italian cities Milan and Venice—appointed special officials to safeguard public health. By 1450, the Milan team included:
- a physician (to prescribe medicines)
- a surgeon (to perform operations)
- a lawyer (to draft new laws)
- a barber (to let blood—believed to cure illness)
- two horsemen (for carrying urgent messages)
- three footmen (to be generally useful)
- two gravediggers.

Sickness and Disease

In the Middle Ages, only 10–15 percent of people inhabited urban areas; the rest lived in the countryside. Sanitation in the crowded towns and cities, as well as in the countryside, was very poor. Most houses did not have plumbing or access to fresh water for bathing and washing.

Indoor toilets were unheard of; people used outside latrines. At night, they used chamber pots, and the contents of these were usually disposed of in the street just outside the house, causing germs to be spread. This lack of hygiene led to a host of killer diseases, including typhoid, typhus, cholera, and dysentery.

Typhoid and cholera spread through communities when human excrement entered the public water supply, while typhus was caused by lice in people's hair and clothes. It didn't always kill its victims, but they remained carriers for the rest of their lives, spreading the disease to people they came in contact with.

Infant Mortality

Physicians in the Middle Ages were fond of saying that they could cure anyone between the ages of seven and 70. Young children of the time were very prone to infections due to malnourishment and lack of hygiene in the home. The first year of a child's life was especially difficult, even more so if the mother could not breastfeed. Many women, especially those of noble birth, were required to produce heirs. As the mortality (death) rate was high, they married in their early teens, which gave them more time to have children, some of whom might live into adulthood. In effect, this meant that many mothers were forced to have babies before they were strong enough to do so. Many women died during childbirth; others produced infants that could not combat infections and disease.

Waste was often poured from people's windows into the street below.

Poor diet and coarse clothing also caused many skin-related conditions, including scurvy, scabies, and scrofula. Inadequate storage of grain was the cause of a terrible disease, St. Anthony's fire, which blistered and deformed its victims before they died. Rancid food was commonly consumed. The bad taste was masked by rich sauces and sweet-smelling herbs, but these did not prevent food poisoning.

Country people did not live in the same cramped conditions as city dwellers, but they faced health hazards nonetheless. Many lived in wooden hovels with thatched roofs, which contained all kinds of vermin. The droppings of rats, birds, and other creatures often ended up in the food of those living below.

For those living close to marshy land and stagnant water, there was another deadly hazard: malaria. Between 900 and 1300, Europe experienced an uncharacteristically warm climate, creating the perfect breeding ground for the mosquito, which carried the disease.

Life for the rich was less fraught with danger. They had access to clean water and bathed regularly, often in heated water to avoid catching pneumonia. The rich could also afford to eat more fresh food and employed cooks trained in the art of preserving fish and meat. If they became sick, the nobility had access to the best medical care available.

Lepers were often required to ring a bell to warn passersby of their presence.

The Leper's Plight
Leprosy, a disease that affects the skin and nerves, was common in the Middle Ages. Since it was highly contagious, victims were isolated in communities, either in abandoned villages or monasteries run by brave monks.
"I forbid you to ever enter a church, a monastery, a fair, a mill, a market, or an assembly of people. I forbid you to leave your house unless dressed in your recognizable garb [clothing] and also shod. I forbid you to wash your hands or to launder anything or to drink at any stream or fountain, unless using your own barrel or dipper ... I command you, if accosted by anyone while on a road, to set yourself downwind of them before you answer. I forbid you to enter any narrow passage, lest a passerby bump against you."
(From the *Mass of Separation*, a thirteenth-century ritual conducted by a priest to officially separate a leper from his community.)

Physicians, Surgeons, and Healers

Sick people in the Middle Ages had access to various medical practitioners and healers, depending on their wealth and where they lived. The rich could consult physicians, who were few in number and mostly based in cities. Physicians trained for five years. Drawn mainly from the ranks of the clergy, their education not only prepared them for practicing medicine, but also equipped them to teach their skills to others. Physicians were the wealthiest and highest-ranking members of the medical community. They rarely conducted physical examinations, preferring to diagnose illnesses by questioning patients or analyzing urine samples.

In this fourteenth-century illustration, a corpse is dissected during an anatomy lesson at the University of Montpellier.

The modern-day barber's pole is a reminder of the previous role of barbers as part-time surgeons.

Surgeons performed most of the operations that physicians considered beneath them, such as setting broken bones and closing wounds. They trained by being apprenticed to other surgeons and relied more on practical experience than books. They delivered babies by cesarean section, treated blood loss, removed gallstones, and performed bloodlettings (cutting a vein to draw out infected blood).

Barbers performed operations on poor people who could not afford to see a surgeon. They also pulled teeth and cut people's hair. Barbers stood well below surgeons in the medical hierarchy. However, by the fifteenth century, their practical knowledge had come to be appreciated, and surgeons reluctantly accepted them as colleagues. Now called barber-surgeons, they had to receive formal training before they could practice. In France, they were required to attend the Faculte de Medicine, where they attended lectures and took an examination.

People who could not afford to see physicians, surgeons, or even barbers could turn to medical practitioners called leeches. Like the barbers, leeches did not have any formal training but performed many of the same duties, although they preferred to use herbal and folk remedies. Some learned their craft by watching and assisting surgeons.

The majority of those living in the countryside only had access to unlicensed herbalists or folk healers. They offered cures ranging from herbs and plants with healing properties to magical charms. Remedies included swallowing spiders encased in raisins to cure ague (fever) and tying bags of buttercups around victims' necks to ward off insanity. Most folk healers were women, and their arts were often passed on from mother to daughter.

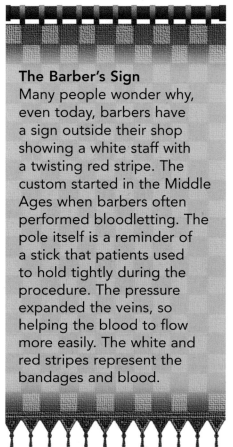

The Barber's Sign
Many people wonder why, even today, barbers have a sign outside their shop showing a white staff with a twisting red stripe. The custom started in the Middle Ages when barbers often performed bloodletting. The pole itself is a reminder of a stick that patients used to hold tightly during the procedure. The pressure expanded the veins, so helping the blood to flow more easily. The white and red stripes represent the bandages and blood.

Having Surgery

Surgery in the Middle Ages was fraught with danger. Many patients remained awake during operations. The majority died of shock or pain before the surgery was finished. There were no antiseptics, and those who survived the ordeal often succumbed to infection afterward.

Surgery was therefore usually performed only as a last resort, when all other treatments had failed. The most common operations were minor ones. Surgeons removed cataracts from eyes, reset broken bones, adjusted dislocated bones, and repaired hernias.

Surgeons often used plants and herbs for pain relief. These included mandragora, the root of the poisonous mandrake plant. Cannabis, opium, and a poisonous herb called deadly

A surgeon places a patient's leg in a splint. The most frequent demand for medical help was for the treatment of injuries.

nightshade were also used. Some surgeons used alcohol or a mixture of mandrake and wine.

The anesthetics were administered by inhalation or drinking. Sometimes a sea sponge called the spongia somnifera was dipped in the wine and held under the patient's nose until he or she passed out. It was difficult for surgeons to gauge the right amount of drug needed for a particular patient. Some would continually tweak a patient's nose during the operation to make sure he or she had not died. Hugh of Lucca, an Italian doctor from the early thirteenth century, would tie his patients to the operating table in case the patient woke up halfway through the surgery.

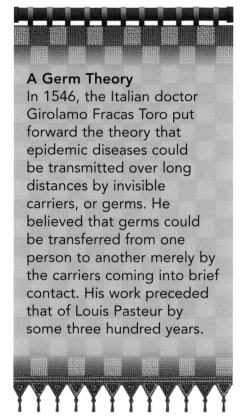

A Germ Theory
In 1546, the Italian doctor Girolamo Fracas Toro put forward the theory that epidemic diseases could be transmitted over long distances by invisible carriers, or germs. He believed that germs could be transferred from one person to another merely by the carriers coming into brief contact. His work preceded that of Louis Pasteur by some three hundred years.

Surgeons also treated injured soldiers on battlefields. They dug bullets out of wounds, sealed torn flesh, and amputated limbs where gangrene had set in. Gunpowder wounds were believed to be poisonous, just like snakebites. Surgeons would sear the wounds by pouring boiling oil into them. They also sealed wounds by applying red-hot pokers to the open flesh. The process burned the skin, so that not enough of it was left to cover over the amputation. As a result, many soldiers either bled to death or died from infection.

An operation is performed on an injured soldier. Battlefield surgeons were skilled at dealing with sword and arrow wounds.

Going to the Dentist

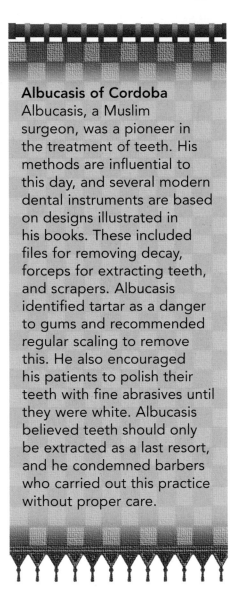

Albucasis of Cordoba
Albucasis, a Muslim surgeon, was a pioneer in the treatment of teeth. His methods are influential to this day, and several modern dental instruments are based on designs illustrated in his books. These included files for removing decay, forceps for extracting teeth, and scrapers. Albucasis identified tartar as a danger to gums and recommended regular scaling to remove this. He also encouraged his patients to polish their teeth with fine abrasives until they were white. Albucasis believed teeth should only be extracted as a last resort, and he condemned barbers who carried out this practice without proper care.

As tooth-drawers did their work, an assistant would play a drum to drown out the customer's cries of pain.

Qualified dentists were called "dentatores." They were trained at universities and were extremely expensive, so few people could afford their services. Dentatores believed that tooth decay was caused by tiny worms in the mouth. They used scrapers to remove rotten parts of teeth and filled cavities with metal fillings, sometimes made of gold. Loose teeth were strengthened with metal bindings. Their array of implements included saws, forceps, and files.

Barber-surgeons were also allowed to pull teeth, and unqualified tooth-drawers were available at fairs and markets all over Europe. They usually wore necklaces strung with teeth to show how many people had trusted them with extractions. They prided themselves on their ability to pull out teeth with as little pain as possible.

Between 700 and 1200, Muslim Arabs made great advances in oral science. They discovered ways to straighten crooked teeth and make false molars from animal bones. This knowledge gradually filtered through to the dentatores of Europe.

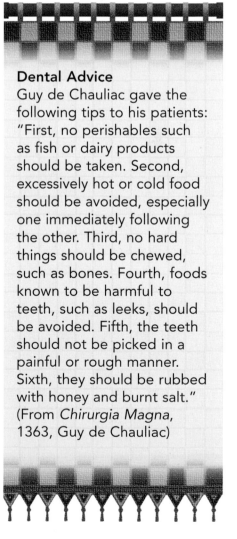

A collection of dental instruments illustrated in Albucasis' famous fourteenth-century medical encyclopedia.

While European barber-surgeons and tooth-drawers concentrated on pulling teeth, enlightened Arab physicians only advocated it if no other option was available. Renowned surgeon Albucasis of Cordoba, who lived from 1013 to 1106, believed that everything should be done to save a broken tooth. In his writings, he gave detailed information on how to bind and repair broken teeth.

Albucasis pioneered many new methods of dentistry, including splinting and bridging teeth. He also advised his patients to brush their teeth with an early form of tooth powder, knowing that oral hygiene kept the gums healthy. His work greatly influenced European dentistry.

In France, a physician named Guy de Chauliac (1300–68) also promoted the importance of oral hygiene in his writings. De Chauliac was the first doctor to refer to dentatores in his work, writing that they were not mere teeth-pullers but qualified professionals who also treated infected tissue in the mouth. In the early 1400s, another dental pioneer, Giovanni de Arcoli, urged people to avoid hot, cold, or sweet foods and was the first to mention the use of gold fillings.

People who could not afford to visit a dentatore, a barber-surgeon, or even a tooth-drawer at the market could see a folk healer. She would let them touch a tooth taken from a dead person. The ritual was supposed to cure their ailment.

Dental Advice

Guy de Chauliac gave the following tips to his patients: "First, no perishables such as fish or dairy products should be taken. Second, excessively hot or cold food should be avoided, especially one immediately following the other. Third, no hard things should be chewed, such as bones. Fourth, foods known to be harmful to teeth, such as leeks, should be avoided. Fifth, the teeth should not be picked in a painful or rough manner. Sixth, they should be rubbed with honey and burnt salt." (From *Chirurgia Magna*, 1363, Guy de Chauliac)

Women in Medieval Medicine

During the Middle Ages, a great many women were involved in the provision of health care and medicine, not just as folk healers, but also as nurses and midwives. Nurses worked mainly in hospitals. Their primary duties involved washing, dressing, and feeding the sick. They were also expected to wash soiled linen and prepare the dead for burial. Most nurses joined a monastic order, dedicating their entire lives to the curing of the sick. Rich people would sometimes hire a nurse to look after a patient at home.

A midwife attends a woman in labor.

Midwives learned their trade by assisting more experienced practitioners. They mixed practical knowledge with superstitious practices inherited from their elders. A good midwife, for example, would have the foresight to use pepper to cause violent sneezing, thus inducing birth. But she might also open all the drawers, doors, and bottles in the room to make sure no evil spirits were hiding there during the birth.

Before midwives could practice, they had to obtain a document from their local parish priest attesting to their good character. A document from 1490, written by a lawyer from Cordoba, details the birth of a nobleman's child. He describes how he searched

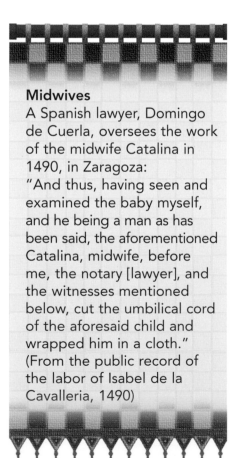

Midwives
A Spanish lawyer, Domingo de Cuerla, oversees the work of the midwife Catalina in 1490, in Zaragoza:
"And thus, having seen and examined the baby myself, and he being a man as has been said, the aforementioned Catalina, midwife, before me, the notary [lawyer], and the witnesses mentioned below, cut the umbilical cord of the aforesaid child and wrapped him in a cloth."
(From the public record of the labor of Isabel de la Cavalleria, 1490)

the two midwives present at the birth to make sure that they had not smuggled another infant into the room under their skirts. He also states that they both took oaths that bound them to deliver the baby safely and "without fraud."

In 1221, the Holy Roman Emperor Fredrick II decreed that no one could practice medicine without a university qualification. This effectively barred women from the profession, since they were forbidden to attend universities.

In 1322, the medical faculty of Paris prosecuted Jacqueline Felicie de Almania for operating without a license. During her trial, she argued that women doctors should be allowed to treat female patients. It was impossible for men to examine them properly, since male doctors could only treat female patients covered by a blanket. The court ignored her plea and banned her.

Some wealthy women did manage to attend medical schools. Of these, the most famous was Trotula, who lived in the early thirteenth century. She was the leader of a group called "the ladies of Salerno." An experienced midwife, she wrote at length about gynecology, obstetrics, birth control, and infertility. Her most influential work was *Passionibus Mulierum Curandorum* (*The Diseases of Women*).

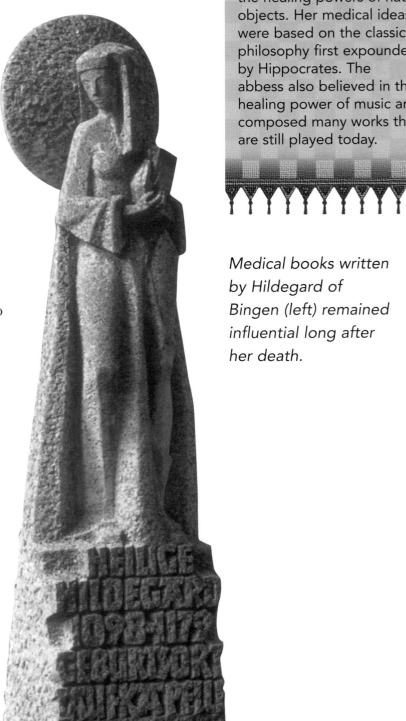

Hildegard of Bingen
Hildegard of Bingen was a German abbess who lived from 1098 to 1179. An educated woman of noble birth, she wrote many books, including *Physica* and *Causae et Curae* (*Causes and Cures*). They were both works about the healing powers of natural objects. Her medical ideas were based on the classical philosophy first expounded by Hippocrates. The abbess also believed in the healing power of music and composed many works that are still played today.

Medical books written by Hildegard of Bingen (left) remained influential long after her death.

Religion in Towns

Most people in medieval European towns followed the Christian faith. Some were devout. They worshiped God, prayed to the saints, and gave generously to charities. Others went to church on holy days, but otherwise did not let their faith greatly affect their daily life. Many medieval people also believed in ancient, pre-Christian magic—such as witches who cast spells, ghosts that walked at Halloween, or spirits that lived in trees.

Whatever people privately believed, the Church as an institution was a powerful force in medieval towns. Church leaders had the right to summon men and women to Church

Multicultural Life

There were communities of Jewish people living in many medieval European towns. In some places, such as Italy, they lived and worked peacefully as respected citizens. But in other countries, such as England, they were persecuted and eventually driven out. Until 1492, southern Spain was governed by Muslim emirs (princes). In the early medieval era, they ruled over a multicultural community based in the city of Cordoba. Here, Muslims, Christians, and Jews from Europe, the Middle East, and North Africa created thriving businesses and great works of art and scholarship. But after 1200, the south of Spain became a battleground, as Muslim and Christian rulers fought for control.

Controversial religious reformer Girolamo Savonarola attracted many followers in Florence, Italy. But his teachings were condemned by Church leaders, and he was tortured, then executed.

This magnificent medieval cathedral towers over the city of Chartres, France. It is now a world heritage site.

courts and punish them for breaking Church laws. These governed all kinds of personal activity, such as telling lies, gossiping, swearing, sex before marriage, and adultery. The Church required everyone to make regular confessions of their sins to a priest and controlled ceremonies that marked the most important stages in their lives, such as baptism, marriage, and funerals.

The Church also had a powerful physical presence in medieval towns. Churches and cathedrals were the largest and most beautiful town buildings. They were built as places of Christian worship and to give glory to God. Some town churches and cathedrals were also places of pilgrimage. They housed relics (physical remains) of Christian saints. Thousands of pilgrims came each year to revere them and to ask the saint for help—for example, to cure them from disease. After around 1300, many towns built huge churches where friars (missionary priests) preached rousing sermons to large congregations of ordinary citizens.

However, fine churches and cathedrals were also proud symbols of a town's wealth and status, and places where local craftworkers could display their skills. Leading families in many cities and towns gave money to help build churches and the family burial places and memorial statues inside them.

Town councils and Church leaders often worked together to control town politics. Usually, they were on the same side against criminals and protesters, but occasionally they became involved in bitter disputes. Church leaders were also in two minds about the morality of big business. They relied on rich merchants for donations, but they also disapproved of lending money with interest (which was how town bankers made their profits) and taught that "Trade can scarcely, if ever, be pleasing to God."

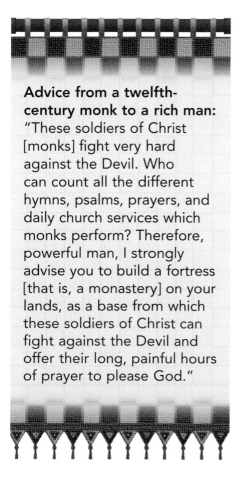

Advice from a twelfth-century monk to a rich man: "These soldiers of Christ [monks] fight very hard against the Devil. Who can count all the different hymns, psalms, prayers, and daily church services which monks perform? Therefore, powerful man, I strongly advise you to build a fortress [that is, a monastery] on your lands, as a base from which these soldiers of Christ can fight against the Devil and offer their long, painful hours of prayer to please God."

Church and Society

It is difficult for us today to understand just how important the Church was to ordinary people in the medieval age. From birth onward, people's lives were governed by the Church. Clergymen (Church officials) baptised infants, controlled the education of children, performed marriage services, and when someone died, they supervised their burial and conducted prayers for their soul.

People generally believed that their conduct while they were alive would determine their destination after death. They thought that those people who died without committing any

A Crusader sets off for the Holy Land, ready to give up his life for the Church.

Jan Hus (circa 1369–1415), a peasant from Bohemia, campaigned against Church corruption and was burned at the stake as a heretic. His death inspired his followers, the Hussites, to take up arms, and war raged in Bohemia until the year 1434.

sins would go to heaven, while those who died without seeking forgiveness would go to hell. They also believed that confessing their sins and asking for forgiveness would grant them a shorter stay in purgatory, a place where those who died went in order to pay for sins that they had confessed to while they were alive.

One way in which people thought that they could reduce their time in purgatory was to contribute money to the Church. Rich men, including kings, noblemen, and merchants, provided the money to build magnificent cathedrals. They did this to pay for their sins and also gain power and influence while they were alive.

The power of the Church was demonstrated in 1095 by the launch of the Crusades. This was a series of military expeditions made by European Christians to retake Palestine, a land sacred to Christians and at that time under Muslim control. Pope Urban II made a speech urging Christian knights to take back the Holy Land. Thousands of men of all classes set off to fight, many of them never to return. They believed that what they were doing was the will of God and that taking part would guarantee their place in heaven.

Heresy

Besides Muslims (also called Saracens), there were other people called heretics who were seen as a threat to medieval Christianity. Heretics were Christians who questioned whether certain Church beliefs and teachings were true. One such group were the Cathars, who believed that everything material—wealth, property, even everyday necessities—was evil. The Hussites were another group who refused to accept the authority of the Pope or that only priests could perform the important religious services. In the early medieval period, heretical groups were generally tolerated. However, from the thirteenth century, heretics were persecuted by a special court known as the Inquisition, and hundreds of people were burned to death for heresy.

Church Business

The Importance of Holy Relics

Holy relics were highly prized items in medieval times. A really wealthy man, such as a king or baron, might have his own personal collection, and churches kept their collections securely locked up. The relic might be the entire remains of a saint or just a fragment of their finger bone, the water a saint's corpse might have been washed in, or a fragment of what was claimed to be the cross on which Christ was crucified. One medieval source tells the story of St. Hugh of Lincoln, who attempted to steal part of a relic from a monastery in France by biting off a piece of the finger of a female saint.

Churches before the medieval age were places where ordinary people tended to go only at Easter, when they were expected to confess their sins and take part in a ritual called communion. The growth of religious belief in the medieval age changed all that. Churches became the heart of the community.

The medieval Church was very much involved in the daily lives of its parishioners. The parish priest was expected to supervise a number of rituals—listening to confession, baptizing babies, blessing marriages, confirming the faith of young people, providing spiritual aid to the dying, and overseeing the burial of the dead. Everyone was expected to attend the ceremony called mass, which took place on Sundays. The Church was also the main source of education for ordinary people. People learned Bible stories from stone carvings and the paintings that decorated church walls. People were taught the penalties of sin and told they would be judged by God after they died.

In the San Guiliano Convent in Italy are the relics (cloak and purse) of St. John of Capistrano (1386–1456).

The Church year began with the 12 days of Christmas that celebrated the birth of Christ. This festival was followed by Shrovetide and then Holy Week. This commemorated the death of Christ and was the most important religious event of the year. Church processions took place, and everyone was expected to take part in the ritual called Holy Communion. Summer was marked in the Christian calendar by Corpus Christi, a celebration of the Church belief that Christ was bodily present in the bread taken at mass. This was also accompanied by religious processions. Finally, the year ended with All Souls' Day and All Saints' Day, when the Church held prayers for the souls of the dead.

Another big business for the Church, especially in the cathedrals and grand town churches, was pilgrimages. In medieval times, people believed they could be cured of an illness if they touched a holy relic. Pilgrims to a shrine that contained the relic of a saint would donate money to the church in exchange for a cure. On a particular saint's day, the church holding a relic of the saint would be crowded with pilgrims.

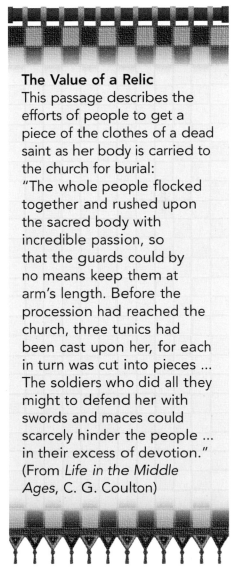

The Value of a Relic
This passage describes the efforts of people to get a piece of the clothes of a dead saint as her body is carried to the church for burial:
"The whole people flocked together and rushed upon the sacred body with incredible passion, so that the guards could by no means keep them at arm's length. Before the procession had reached the church, three tunics had been cast upon her, for each in turn was cut into pieces ... The soldiers who did all they might to defend her with swords and maces could scarcely hinder the people ... in their excess of devotion."
(From *Life in the Middle Ages*, C. G. Coulton)

Entertainments

Mystery Plays
In English, French, and German towns, popular entertainments included "mystery plays" performed by members of craft guilds. In spite of their name, they were not detective dramas! They were named after the French word for skilled trade, which was *métier*. Mystery plays grew out of earlier medieval dramas performed in churches. They retold Bible stories but set them in the everyday medieval world, so ordinary people could understand their message and enjoy them.

Medieval townspeople worked hard, but they also enjoyed many days off, when they could relax. Originally, most of their holidays were Church festivals (our word "holiday" comes from "holy-day"), such as Christmas, Easter, and saints days. The Church hoped that men and women would use this time for prayer and religious study, but holidays soon became a time for entertainments of a nonreligious kind as well.

A rich lord would show off his wealth by entertaining guests at his castle. A grand feast, or banquet, would be provided. The lord and lady would sit at the high table, and each new course would be heralded by a trumpet, played as the food was brought in. Sometimes their food would be tasted for them by a servant to check that it had not been poisoned. After dining, a jester would tell jokes and a group of minstrels played music.

At Christmas time, groups of actors called mummers put on masks and monster costumes, sang and danced, fought mock battles, and acted simple plays based on exciting stories from saints' lives (such as St. George, who killed a dragon) or ancient legends about mysterious nature spirits like the Green Man. Old, pre-Christian festivals were also celebrated in many towns,

Medieval musicians played lively tunes for dancing on bagpipes (left), shawms (middle), and drums (right).

for example, by decorating houses with green garlands on May Day and lighting bonfires at midsummer (June 21).

Throughout the year, citizens looked forward to regular visits from roaming entertainers. These included jugglers, acrobats, animal trainers, and fools—who told rude jokes and mocked powerful people. Musicians performed songs and dance tunes on fiddles, bagpipes, nackers (small drums), shawms (very loud reed instruments similar to oboes), or the pipe and tabor. This was an early kind of one-man band. It consisted of a pipe on which tunes were played with the left hand and a flat drum, hit with the right hand.

All year round, less active amusements included board games such as chess and playing cards (both introduced to Europe by Muslims) and dice. Medieval people liked to bet on these and also on wrestling matches, bearbaiting (fights between fierce dogs and bears), and contests between fighting cocks (roosters). Most people today would find these last two entertainments very bloodthirsty and cruel.

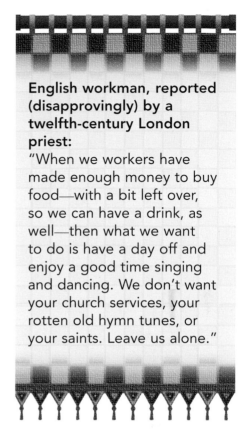

English workman, reported (disapprovingly) by a twelfth-century London priest:
"When we workers have made enough money to buy food—with a bit left over, so we can have a drink, as well—then what we want to do is have a day off and enjoy a good time singing and dancing. We don't want your church services, your rotten old hymn tunes, or your saints. Leave us alone."

Spanish noble ladies play chess, 1282. They are sitting in an elegant building decorated in Spanish Muslim style.

Under Attack

Towns as well as castles were vulnerable to attack. Strong walls and gates could keep out enemies, but towns were still in danger of being besieged. During a siege, hostile troops camped outside a town, surrounded its walls and gates, and

Medieval soldiers besiege a town around 1450. They are armed with longbows and cannons.

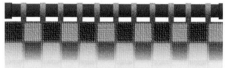

Town Punishments
"If bakers and brewers break the Assize of Bread and Beer [laws about weights, measures, and quality] one, two, or three times, they shall be fined. But if they go on breaking the law, then a baker shall be put in a pillory and a brewer in a tumbrel."

Pillory: a tall wooden frame that was fixed around the neck and hands. Lawbreakers were locked in the pillory, and townspeople threw rotten food and other garbage at them.

Tumbrel: a wooden sled or low cart with wheels. Lawbreakers were tied onto this and dragged roughly through the streets, while townspeople jeered at them.

refused to let anyone in or out. Eventually, all food in the town was eaten and citizens starved. At the same time, enemy soldiers used massive "siege engines," such as battering rams, to try and smash through castle walls, shot spears and arrows at town defenders, and hurled dead bodies back into the town to spread grief and fear. After around 1400, they also used cannons that fired iron shot to attack town walls.

Town treasures, such as gold crosses in churches, fine furnishings in merchant houses, or valuable goods in warehouses, were all rich pickings for invaders. On many occasions, army leaders were unable to control their troops once they had forced their way into a town. Soldiers looted all they could, destroyed all the rest, and brutally attacked peaceful citizens.

Because of these dangers, even in peacetime, all "foreigners" (noncitizens) had to identify themselves to guards on duty at town gates and give a good reason for wanting to enter the town. Town gates were kept locked from dusk to dawn, and councils imposed a curfew. This meant that no foreigner was allowed out of their house after dark—on pain of being arrested as a spy.

Town councils also worried about rowdy protests by young apprentices, who complained about low pay and poor working conditions, and violent riots by poor people, who resented the vast gap between them and the richest citizens of the town. Councils appointed watchmen to patrol the streets and keep a lookout for trouble. They set up community-based schemes to report criminals, such as pickpockets, burglars, and confidence tricksters, who found many victims in towns. They held courts to try all these offenders and also to punish traders who damaged the town's good name by cheating customers.

Many features of medieval town life still survive today. We still have town mayors and town councillors, open-air markets, streets lined with stores, fine town houses, and crowded slums. In some parts of Europe, medieval towns have been carefully preserved as heritage centers and tourist attractions. We can still see their churches, merchant homes, city walls, and narrow, winding streets and feel what it was like to live in medieval times.

Laws of Maldon, Essex, 1468:
- Every foreigner must be indoors by 10 p.m. in the summer and 8 p.m. in the winter.
- The bailiffs [town council officers] will punish all "naughty brawlers."
- If one man attacks another and draws blood, he will be fined.
- No foreigner shall carry a weapon in the town.
- Anyone who puts dung or rubbish on the public road shall be fined.
- Any pig wandering loose in the streets may be caught and sold, the money will go to the town.
- Any councillor who stirs up quarrels at council meetings will be fined.
- No burgess may call a council officer "thief, knave, backbiter, whoreson [son of a prostitute], false, forsworn [breaker of promises], cuckold [man whose wife is unfaithful], or bawd [immoral]."

The Doge (elected ruler) of Venice, Italy, discusses city politics with top churchmen, while scribes (trained writers) make a careful record of their words.

Timeline

330	Roman Empire divides. Constantinople (now Istanbul) becomes capital. Grows into greatest city in Europe.
476	Last Roman emperor leaves Rome.
ca. 600–700	New trading towns ("wics") set up on either side of North Sea.
750	Vikings set up trading post at Staria Ladoga (now in northern Russia).
794	Frankish Emperor Charlemagne reforms coins, weights, and measures throughout his empire to encourage trade.
822	Two cities, Novgorod and Kiev, unite to form first Russian state.
849–99	King Alfred the Great of Wessex, England, builds burghs (fortified towns) to defend his kingdom..
980	Birth of Muslim scholar Avicenna, who wrote the Book of Healing and the Canon of Medicine.
ca. 1000	Cordoba, in Muslim Spain, is a great multicultural place of art, trade, and learning.
1013	Birth of Albucasis, perhaps the greatest surgeon of the Middle Ages.
ca. 1075–1122	Italian towns win right to govern themselves.
ca. 1100–1300	The Church builds hospitals in towns; town councils make laws to improve cleanliness and public health.
ca. 1160	Northern European cities build churches and cathedrals in soaring Gothic style.
ca. 1175–1250	Great age of international trade fairs in Champagne region, France.
ca. 1200–1500	Universities built in many European towns.
1204	Venice, Italy, controls shipping and trade in Mediterranean Sea.
1252	Rich Italian city of Florence makes first gold coins for almost 500 years—a sign that trade is flourishing.

1259	Northern European trading towns on shore of Baltic Sea join together in a powerful "Hansa" (league).
1265	Representatives of boroughs (towns) become members of English parliament.
1277–95	King Edward I of England founds 10 new towns in Wales to control conquered land.
1277	Genoa, Italy, sets up trading route between Mediterranean and North Sea.
1309	First town clock in Europe, in Milan, Italy.
ca. 1340	Around 15 cities in Europe now have over 50,000 inhabitants.
1347–51	Black Death kills around one-third of Europe's population. Temporary collapse of trade.
1420–1600	Italian cities rebuilt in splendid Renaissance style.
1445–55	First Bible printed, in city of Mainz, Germany.
1453	Constantinople conquered by Muslim Ottoman Turks.

Waging War in the Middle Ages

Cut and Thrust

The following lines, translated by William Caxton in 1489, describe the advantage of a rapier or thrusting sword over a cutting sword:

"And for this reason also is the stroke of a foyne [sword] better and surer because he that smites [strikes] with the edge in heaving up of both his arms shows himself naked and bare and discovered along his right side and this does not he that smites with a foyne but keeps himself close as he strikes and may hurt his enemy before that other heaves up his arms for to smite with the edge."
(From *The Book of Fayttes of Armes and of Chyvalrye*, Christine de Pisan)

Warfare was common in medieval Europe, although perhaps no more common than in any other period. After the breakup of the western Roman Empire, the Frankish tribes occupying most of the area that is now France and Germany gradually evolved a way of producing armies. Armored warriors mounted on horseback were given land in return for fighting. This was part of the feudal system, with the king or duke at the top, and developed at first especially in France. It allowed armies to be recruited to fight as part of the soldiers' service to their lord.

This situation slowly changed in the thirteenth and fourteenth centuries, when recruiting soldiers via agreed contracts became more popular. This produced more professional armies, rather than bands of men who wanted to go home when their length of feudal service ran out.

A late fifteenth-century battle scene shows French cavalry charging a hedge of spearheads presented by English soldiers.

Alongside these soldiers were mercenaries, hired fighting men who stayed as long as they were paid. Often brutal and disliked—for example, the Flemish crossbowmen hired by England's King John—mercenaries played an important role in medieval armies.

Many wars occurred during the medieval period. Some caused great changes, such as the Norman Conquest of England in 1066. Some saw great loss of life for little gain, such as the Hundred Years War between England and France, which was fought on and off from 1337 to 1453. In Spain, the Catholic kings wrested control of the country from the Muslims who had settled there. This "Reconquest" was finally completed in 1492.

In eastern Europe, the native Slavs fought the German Teutonic Knights who had settled there and had forced them to become Christians, while the Slavs in fifteenth-century Bohemia (part of the modern Czech Republic) revolted against the German Holy Roman Empire. The Swiss forced out the Austrians who tried to take over their mountainous country, and in fourteenth and fifteenth-century Italy, mercenary armies, the condottieri, held sway in the powerful cities.

During this time, the race was on between armor and weapons—armorers tried to produce the best protection for soldiers, and smiths tried to make weapons that could get through the armor's defenses.

Ambush!
At the Battle of Maclodio in 1427, Venetians attacked a Milanese camp but deliberately sent in a half-hearted attack that was easily beaten off. The Venetian condottieri (mercenary forces in Italy) lured the Milanese to pursue them and feigned a retreat into the marshes. Caught on narrow causeways with their retreat cut off, the Milanese were ambushed and shot down. On surrendering, huge numbers of prisoners were taken for the price of a few Venetian dead.

This hand-and-a-half sword, probably made in Italy, dates from 1400 (top), and a cutting sword dates from about 1100.

Eleventh Century Arms

These mailed Norman knights are depicted in the Bayeux Tapestry.

The time of the Norman Conquest of England was the age of mail, or chain mail. Mail was made of thousands of interlinked iron rings. The mail coat varied in length depending on a man's wealth. Short coats reached the hips, but many soldiers wore coats down to the knees, split at the front and back for ease of movement and to allow a knight to mount his horse. Most coats had elbow-length sleeves, and many also had mail hoods to protect the head.

The mail was flexible, but this meant it bent inward when struck, sometimes causing severe bruising or broken bones even if the rings had not been penetrated. For this reason, it is likely that a padded coat was worn beneath.

Lethal Weapon
The long, two-handed ax had a cutting edge made from especially hardened steel welded onto the blade. It was a fearsome weapon and was said to be able to cut through a horse and rider with one blow.

Soldiers also carried a large wooden shield. The shield did not bend when hit, although it could be split. The older style of shield was circular and sometimes dished like a bowl. A hand hole was cut out of the middle to allow the fist to grip a carrying bar, and this gap was covered at the front by a metal cup called a boss. By the middle of the eleventh century, however, many soldiers were carrying instead a large kite-shaped or "teardrop" shield held by straps. Many shields were covered in leather to make them tougher.

The conical helmet was made from either one piece or several segments, sometimes reinforced by bands. A noseguard also helped stop a slashing blow from reaching the upper face. Poorer warriors often had only a shield, while long-range archers did not even have a spear.

The warrior's chosen weapon was his sword. This had a double-edged blade used mainly for cutting at an opponent. Down the middle of each side ran a channel called a fuller, which was designed to reduce the weight without weakening the blade. Many swords were made from a mixture of iron and steel: the iron to make them tough and flexible, the steel to give them hard cutting edges. A weight on the end of the hilt, behind the hand, acted as a counterbalance to make the balancing point as close to the hand as possible, so that the sword was not too blade-heavy.

Mounted knights carried a light spear called a lance, but many soldiers also carried either light javelins or ones with larger stabbing blades. Vikings favored axes, some with blades over 10 inches wide mounted on long wooden handles. Archers used wooden bows measuring almost 6.5 feet long. Crossbows were simple weapons with wooden bow arms.

A dismounted Norman knight wears mail hauberk and carries a kite-shaped shield. Similar armor was worn by most western knights.

The Battle of Hastings
These lines, written in about 1073–4, describe the attack mounted by Duke William's Norman soldiers on the English line at the Battle of Hastings in 1066:
"The fighting which followed was most unusual, for one side continued the attack in a series of charges and individual assaults, while the other stood firm as if rooted to the ground ... The Normans shot their arrows, brandished their swords, transfixed the enemy with their spears ..."
(From *The History of William, Duke of the Normans and King of the English*, William of Poitiers)

The Twelfth and Thirteenth Centuries

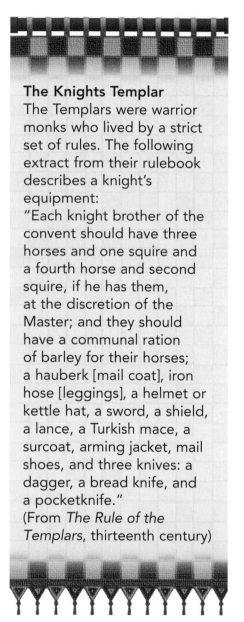

This mid-thirteenth-century knight is wearing a helm and surcoat.

The coat of mail remained the best protection for knights and for others who could afford it, and at first, it changed little. Long sleeves, rare in the eleventh century, gradually became more common. By about 1170, some sleeves extended to form mail mittens called mufflers. The muffler had a slit in the leather palm so the soldier could push his hand out, leaving the muffler hanging at the wrist. A thin cord threaded through the rings could be adjusted to keep the mail from bagging out over the hand. Mail leggings also became popular, either as a strip down the front of the leg or as a full stocking tied up to the belt, with a leather sole under the foot. Padded coats are now mentioned under mail, but ordinary soldiers often wore them alone.

From about 1140, some knights began wearing a long cloth surcoat over their armor, perhaps copied from Muslim dress seen in the Crusades.

Shields became smaller and designed with a straight top edge to allow the soldier to see over but remain protected. The conical

A mid-twelfth-century Templar knight carries the Templar banner.

helmet remained in use throughout this period, but other types also became popular. Round-topped and cylindrical helmets had appeared by about 1200, some fitted with a faceguard something like a welding mask. By 1250, these had developed into a flat-topped helmet that covered the whole head, but they could become very hot. Plates of steel, whalebone, or leather hardened by boiling (called cuir-bouilli) were very slowly being added to exposed parts of the body, usually the knees and shins, in the late thirteenth century.

The sword remained the prized weapon of the knight, and at first, it did not change much, remaining a cutting weapon with sharp edges. However, in the thirteenth century, the hand-and-a-half-sword emerged—this had a longer hilt with room for both hands, making it easier to swing at an opponent. This sword could deal heavy blows.

The French developed another new style with a more pointed blade for thrusting and bursting open mail rings. A short horseman's ax appeared, and occasionally a bronze-headed mace was used like a club. The longbow made its presence felt in the twelfth century, and crossbows were becoming more common by then.

The Kettle Hat
An open helmet with a wide brim appeared in the mid-twelfth century—the kettle hat. It was named after the word for a cauldron. Ideal for deflecting missiles in a siege, it was even used by some knights because it allowed air to reach the face. It was still seen in the form of the British "tin hat" from World War II.

73

The Age of Change

The fourteenth century saw the greatest development in armor. In 1300, a knight wore mainly mail; by 1400, he was often defended by steel plates all over his body.

In the late thirteenth century, a new defense had been introduced, the coat-of-plates, or "plates." This was a jacket either put on over the head like a poncho or laced at the front or the side. Attached to it with rivets, usually on the inside, were metal plates. The rivet heads could be seen on the outside. By the fourteenth century, the coat-of-plates had become very common, usually worn under the surcoat and over the mail. A padded tunic was usually worn under the mail as well, so wearing armor made soldiers feel very hot. During the fourteenth century, the steel (or whalebone or leather) plates multiplied over the arms and legs, and were shaped to fit. By 1400, a separate breastplate had developed.

Tournament Armor
Special jousting equipment began to develop. The frog-mouthed helm was so-called because the lower edge of the vision slit began jutting out to deflect a lance point or the splintered pieces of its shaft. For jousts of peace that used blunted lances, the shield began to be tied to the left side of the breast, and separate breastplates, with a bracket to stop the lance running back after a strike, are first mentioned.

Sir Geoffrey Luttrell receives his crested helm from his wife to wear over a small basinet in about 1335.

A new form of open-faced helmet also developed, known as the basinet. This took the form of either a small cap or a tall cone. At first, it was worn over the mail hood. Later, it began to be attached to the mail itself, and the mail became simply a neck guard. The basinet often had a pointed visor at the front to deflect weapon points.

In the first half of the century, the surcoat became shorter and often quite tight; sometimes it was a thickly padded defense called a gambeson. The shield had become still smaller, and some knights had stopped carrying a shield altogether.

More and more swords were now being made with sharp points, some having sharp edges for cutting and a sharp point for thrusting. Some also had a raised ridge running down the blade to stiffen it for a rigid lunge. Larger swords continued as before, used for battering a man to the ground.

A dagger was a popular addition. It would be carried on the opposite hip to the sword. Daggers had a short, rigid blade for stabbing between joints or through mail.

Steel-headed maces were designed with solid ridges to concentrate the blow at one point in hopes of breaking the opponent's armor. The longbow remained a lethal weapon, but crossbows, though slower, were increasing their power.

A great helm dates from about 1370. The holes at the bottom are for a chain, which kept it from being lost in battle.

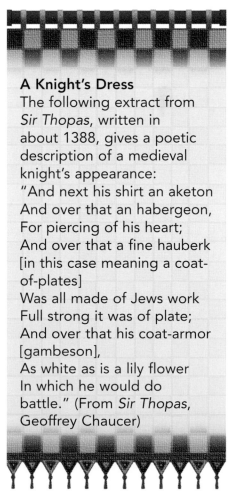

A Knight's Dress
The following extract from *Sir Thopas*, written in about 1388, gives a poetic description of a medieval knight's appearance:
"And next his shirt an aketon
And over that an habergeon,
For piercing of his heart;
And over that a fine hauberk
[in this case meaning a coat-of-plates]
Was all made of Jews work
Full strong it was of plate;
And over that his coat-armor [gambeson],
As white as is a lily flower
In which he would do battle." (From *Sir Thopas*, Geoffrey Chaucer)

Into the Fifteenth Century

Full plate armor finally emerged in the fifteenth century. The pieces were no longer attached inside a cloth covering, and the shining surfaces gave it the name of "alwite" harness, or "all white" armor. The pieces were hinged, or held together with leather straps, or simply riveted together.

The basinet with its mail collar gradually gave way to the great basinet, the mail being replaced by steel plates attached to the basinet itself, making it difficult to turn the head.
The armor was so well designed that a shield was rarely carried, and as most knights now fought on foot, this meant that a long staff weapon could be held in both hands.

By the middle of the fifteenth century, the great armor-making centers of northern Italy, Germany, and Flanders were each producing their own styles of armor. North Italian armor tended

An early-fifteenth-century knight mounts his horse in full plate armor.

to be smooth and rounded, often with only mail over the feet. The typical Italian helmet, the armet, usually completely covered the head and face, with side openings to allow it to be put on.

By contrast, later fifteenth-century German armor was less rounded and more streamlined, with vertical ridges on the surface that helped strengthen the metal and guide weapon points away. The Germans' typical helmet was the sallet, extending to a point at the back to protect the neck and adding a chin defense at the front.

Flemish and other northwestern European workshops used a style similar to the Italian armor but with some German influences, such as the ridges on the plates and a preference for the sallet rather than the Italian style of helmet.

Cut-and-thrust swords with pointed tips and sharp edges remained in use, especially at the beginning of the fifteenth century, but short, rigid blades were increasingly seen, and the larger hand-and-a-half sword was also used on foot.

Staff weapons with long wooden handles were also increasing in popularity. One of the favorites was the poleax (from the word "poll" for head). This was a three-way weapon: It had an ax blade at the top on one side, a hammer facing the other way, and a spike sticking straight up. All three parts of the poleax were designed to crack open armor or dent it out of shape to prevent it from working properly. The halberd had an ax blade with a hook at the back for tripping up opponents or pulling them over.

This late fifteenth-century northwestern European armor shows a sallet without a bevor (chin protector). The soldier carries a poleax.

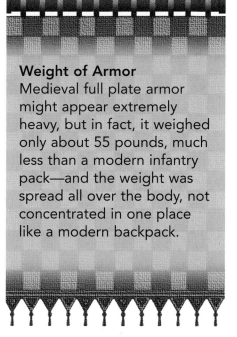

Weight of Armor
Medieval full plate armor might appear extremely heavy, but in fact, it weighed only about 55 pounds, much less than a modern infantry pack—and the weight was spread all over the body, not concentrated in one place like a modern backpack.

77

Armor of Many Types

Mail and plate armor were not the only forms of protection in use. Other materials were useful in creating armor, especially for the less wealthy soldier.

A basic defense, and perhaps the easiest to obtain, was soft or padded armor, made either by taking two layers of cloth and stuffing them with wool, tow (untwisted fibers), or old rags, or by putting together many layers of cloth. This was then quilted to keep it all in place. A tunic made in this way was known as an aketon, gambeson, or pourpoint. For ordinary soldiers, it might be their only armor. Padded armor, usually the gambeson, was sometimes worn over other armor like a surcoat. By the fifteenth century, a shorter version of padded body defense was known as a jack. It was surprisingly effective at stopping a weapon.

These baggage wagons are packed with armor, from about 1250. The left-hand pikeman wears a padded aketon and kettle hat; the far right-hand man may have a curie.

Some soft leather armor was used, but most was cuir-bouilli, leather hardened by boiling or soaking in water or oil to form a very strong, rigid defense. The leather might be tooled with decorative designs and was much cheaper than steel plates. It was probably already used in the thirteenth century for some body defenses strapped together under the mail coat, known as the curie from the French word for leather. As plate limb defenses became common, so cuir-bouilli might be used instead of steel. It seems to have become less common in the fifteenth century.

Whalebone was occasionally carved to make shaped armor plates, mainly in the thirteenth and fourteenth centuries.

As we have seen, the coat-of-plates was a jacket lined with plates often worn over mail. In the fourteenth century, a similar piece of armor known as the brigandine evolved. Small pieces of plate were attached on the inside of a front-fastening canvas jacket, with the rivet heads showing at the front, running in rows across the jacket. The canvas was usually covered with dyed cloth, and the rivet heads were sometimes gilded to make an attractive finish. Rich knights might even wear a brigandine for protection in civilian life.

The Padded Tunic
The following lines describe English soldiers as observed by an Italian writer in 1483: "Indeed, the common soldiery have more comfortable tunics that reach down below the loins and are stuffed with tow [untwisted fibers] or some other material. They say that the softer the tunics, the better do they withstand the blows of arrows and swords, and besides that, in summer they are lighter and in winter more serviceable than iron." (From *The Usurpation of Richard III*, Dominic Mancini)

A fifteenth-century crossbowman wears a brigandine and open sallet.

79

The Making of Armor and Weapons

Producing arms and armor was a skilled process undertaken by swordsmiths and armorers. In the great manufacturing centers, such as northern Italy, hundreds of plate armors were produced every year in the fifteenth century.

Mail wire was wound around a rod and cut down one side to produce a batch of open rings. Each ring had its ends flattened and pierced; then, after interlinking it with four others, the ends of the ring were overlapped and a tiny rivet pushed through the holes in the flattened ends and hammered flat to secure it. In a few cases, a row of riveted rings was linked to a row of rings closed by welding.

It is likely that apprentices did the boring work of producing the rings, and the master mail maker then assembled them into a garment. By adding or subtracting rings from a row, as in knitting, the shape could be varied. Under the armpits, where rings could bunch and knot, a ring might be left out to allow the arm to move.

Plate armor began life as sheets of impure steel. Templates may have been used to draw the shape

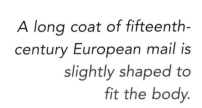

A long coat of fifteenth-century European mail is slightly shaped to fit the body.

This mid-thirteenth-century illustration shows an armorer beating a helm into shape, while a swordsmith checks a blade. Note the mail-covered warhorse.

of a piece of armor on the flat sheet. Large special shears for cutting metal were then used to cut the rough shape. The steel was beaten to the correct shape over an anvil or over smaller, mushroom-headed anvils called stakes. The metal was either worked cold or heated in a furnace to the exact temperature required. Afterward, the edge might be turned over a length of wire to remove any sharpness. The surface was smoothed by grinding and then polished. Rivets, leather straps, and buckles, as well as linings, were added.

Swords carried a certain mystique, partly because the smiths often kept their methods secret. Early blades were made by twisting iron rods and forging them together, the constant folding and beating leaving a pattern on the smooth metal. These were called pattern-welded blades. Steel was added to increase hardness and sharpness to the more supple iron. Heated blades were plunged into a cold liquid, such as oil or water, to help the hardening process. A wooden or horn grip might be added. This was often bound in cloth, leather, or wire to help give a secure grip.

Armor Decoration

Early helmets were decorated with jewels or were painted. In the fourteenth century, a few plate armor pieces had pieces of decorative brass added. By the 1400s, some pieces were engraved by scratching on a design with a sharp instrument called a burin. At the end of the fifteenth century, etching with mild acid had become the main way to decorate armor. Gold was mixed with dangerous mercury that was chased off by heating to leave the gold sealed on the armor.

Arming a Knight

A suit of fifteenth-century plate armor was designed for maximum movement and maximum protection. Plates moved with one another in three ways. Some plates were connected by leather straps riveted on the inner side, some pivoted around a rivet, and a few gave extra movement as the rivet in one plate slid along a slot in the next plate.

An arming doublet was worn under plate armor. This was like a civilian jacket but had mail panels under each armpit and down the inside of the arm to fill the gaps between the plates. The doublet also had strong laces attached to it for tying the pieces of armor—without the doublet, a man could not be armed.

Armor was put on from the feet upward. The sabbaton was a metal overshoe made from steel strips hinged at both sides to allow the foot to bend. The lower leg armor (greave) was hinged like a book to open over the shin and calf; the sabbaton was connected by a lace to its bottom edge. The cuisse and poleyn for thigh and knee were hinged together. They were strapped around the back of the leg and secured to the doublet. The breast and back plates, with hanging skirts, were hinged with pins on the left and buckled together on the right.

A late fifteenth-century knight is armed for foot combat in a tournament.

A fifteenth-century knight is armed by two assistants. The vambrace is being laced at the top of his arm.

The arms were covered with armguards (vambraces), tied by points from the doublet. Above the vambraces, the shoulder pieces (pauldrons) were tied on, and below the vambraces, metal gloves called gauntlets protected the hands.

The helmet was added last to reduce the buildup of heat. Spurs were worn only if the knight would be riding. The sword was belted on, and the knight might also carry a second weapon.

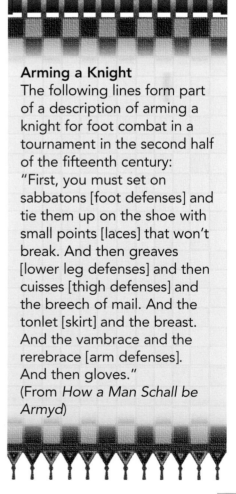

Arming a Knight
The following lines form part of a description of arming a knight for foot combat in a tournament in the second half of the fifteenth century:
"First, you must set on sabbatons [foot defenses] and tie them up on the shoe with small points [laces] that won't break. And then greaves [lower leg defenses] and then cuisses [thigh defenses] and the breech of mail. And the tonlet [skirt] and the breast. And the vambrace and the rerebrace [arm defenses]. And then gloves."
(From *How a Man Schall be Armyd*)

83

Into Battle

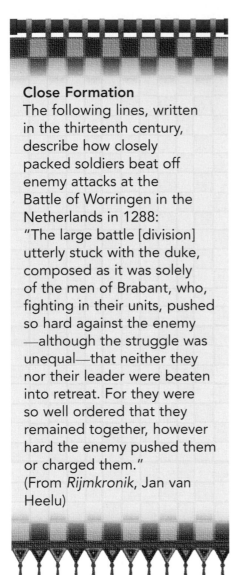
In the eleventh century, most knights fought on horseback, supported by foot soldiers that included archers and some crossbowmen. The knights charged in groups following their lord's pennon, throwing, stabbing, or leveling their lances. Foot soldiers either went ahead of the horsemen with archers to soften up the enemy, or they formed a screen to protect the knights.

The knights' charge was difficult to stop, especially when, after about 1100, large, tightly packed groups advanced together, all lowering their lances at the same time and producing an effect like a steamroller. At Arsuf in 1191, during the Third Crusade, Richard I used his infantry (foot soldiers) and archers as a screen, hoping to draw Saladin's swift horse archers closer to allow his knights to charge before they could gallop clear.

In the late thirteenth century, the Scots tried using infantry with long spears or pikes, forming a "hedgehog" of points called a schiltron, against which horses refused to charge. Archers could be used to break up these massed ranks of men. But at Bannockburn in 1314, the English archers were caught off guard by the Scots cavalry (mounted knights).

Fifteenth-century armored and mounted men-at-arms charge with lowered lances, from the Rout of San Romano.

Increasingly, English armies fought mainly on foot, using bodies of men-at-arms with larger and larger groups of archers, all ideally standing in a protected position to make the enemy charge. First used against the Scots, it was a technique that also proved successful in France during the Hundred Years War, producing such victories as Crécy in 1346 (mainly against cavalry) and Agincourt in 1415 (mainly against infantry). But it did not always work: If the English were caught out of position, they could be routed, as at Patay in 1429.

By the fifteenth century, many men-at-arms only used their warhorses on certain occasions, such as when pursuing fleeing opponents. After the Hundred Years War, longbowmen were ranged against each other in England in the Wars of the Roses. Flemish foot soldiers won a surprising victory over the French at Courtrai in 1302 when they attacked the mounted French knights with clubs and surrounded them. In fifteenth-century Bohemia (part of the present-day Czech Republic), the Slavs in revolt used rings of wagons fitted with guns and homemade flails to beat off the armored knights of the occupying German Empire.

In fourteenth- and fifteenth-century Switzerland, and later also in Germany, ordinary soldiers formed units of specially trained pikemen (infantry carrying spears), who not only stopped cavalry but also fought other pike formations. They became valued as hired soldiers or mercenaries.

A Knight's Ransom
Knights were richer than many other soldiers. On the battlefield, they were more use alive than dead, as they could be held for ransom. Their friends and family would pay large amounts for their return. But in the English Wars of the Roses, old grudges led to nobles being killed in revenge.

Above is a late fifteenth-century woodcut of a German laager, or wagon camp.

Under Siege

Surprise Entry

At Château-Gaillard in 1203–4, the French were having difficulty taking the second of the castle's three courtyards. Suddenly, a soldier noticed a disused toilet shaft and climbed up it to let his friends in. They made such a noise that the English defenders panicked, and the Frenchmen were able to open the gates for their friends.

In medieval warfare, sieges were more common than battles. Battles were terribly risky: You might be killed or lose your lands. It was much safer to attack an enemy's lands and the manors that tended them. Castles gave local protection and forced an invader to capture each one or leave an enemy in his rear as he advanced.

Sieges were sometimes quite formal, with the besieger's heralds demanding surrender or setting the constable a deadline for a decision. Depending on the strength of a castle or town, the besieger might then circle it with men and with ditches or fences, cut it off from food supplies and keep anyone from getting out. If he had time, he could then sit and hope to starve out the defenders, if disease did not break out in his own camp first. Sometimes, he built siege castles, structures of earth and wood filled with soldiers, to watch the enemy while the main besieging army moved on.

Pictured is a late fifteenth-century siege. Cannons are brought up close to bombard the walls with stone shot.

Perhaps the most lethal weapon was the underground mine. The besiegers dug a tunnel under a wall, replacing the excavated foundations with wooden props. Once the miners were clear, the props would be set alight, bringing the wall down as they burned away.

Battering rams were also used: large tree trunks swung from beneath movable sheds. Missiles were shot into the besieged castle. Some catapults used twisted bundles of rope, sinew, or hair to force the throwing arm up. The trebuchet, however, had a large weighted box at one end of a pivoting arm and the missile at the other; when the box pulled one end down, the other lifted and released the missile. Some used a team of men on ropes instead of a box.

Another weapon was the ballista, a giant crossbow that shot large bolts to skewer enemy troops. The ballista was very useful as an antipersonnel weapon, especially when placed near doorways to keep defenders from rushing out to attack the besiegers' camp. Using ladders to climb over the walls was very hazardous, so siege towers might be built to launch men across a wooden bridge onto the battlements in groups. But siege towers were slow-moving and could be burned or damaged by missiles.

If a castle or town had refused to surrender and was then captured, the fate of the defenders lay with the commander of the besieging army. Sometimes, soldiers were allowed to march out as worthy opponents, but often the place was sacked and the defenders executed.

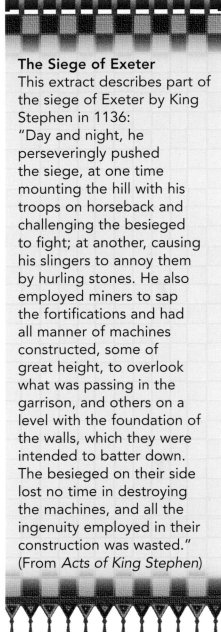

The Siege of Exeter
This extract describes part of the siege of Exeter by King Stephen in 1136:
"Day and night, he perseveringly pushed the siege, at one time mounting the hill with his troops on horseback and challenging the besieged to fight; at another, causing his slingers to annoy them by hurling stones. He also employed miners to sap the fortifications and had all manner of machines constructed, some of great height, to overlook what was passing in the garrison, and others on a level with the foundation of the walls, which they were intended to batter down. The besieged on their side lost no time in destroying the machines, and all the ingenuity employed in their construction was wasted."
(From *Acts of King Stephen*)

This reconstruction of a large trebuchet shows a sling lying in a trough, ready to launch.

A Knight's Steed

Horses were a highly valued part of a knight's equipment. A knight might be busy with his weapon in his right hand and shield in his left, so he had to be able to use his legs and body to control the powerful warhorse. A curb bit, which was like a lever, allowed good control of the horse's head, while long stirrups and a high back and front board on the saddle meant that a knight was literally standing in the stirrups and held in his seat.

Until the twelfth century, horses do not seem to have been provided with any protection at all. Then, in about 1150, a few were provided with a cloth covering at the front and rear that reached down to conceal part of their legs. The front extended upward to form a hood. The cloth probably helped catch weapons, but some coverings may also have been made from padded material. These coats were sometimes made of mail and must have been quite heavy when worn over a cloth version for comfort.

After about 1200, a few horses began to wear a chamfron (solid protection for the head), made either of steel or of cuir bouilli. Such armor remained the main protection, and many warhorses still wore none at all.

A thirteenth-century warhorse wears chamfron and cloth caparison. Note the high saddle boards.

A late fifteenth-century German armored knight is shown on horseback in full Gothic armor.

In the fourteenth century, as plate armor for knights became more usual, horse armor increased. The chamfron might join to neck armor, and occasionally a defense called the peytral was strapped around the horse's chest. By 1400, some also had plate armor for the rump.

For the well-to-do knight in the later fifteenth century, the horse's flanks near the rider's legs might have a plate suspended on either side to fill the gap. This complete armor was very rare, however, and many horses were still given no protection. A complete plate horse armor might weigh about 55–77 pounds and would be lined for comfort.

The Warhorse
The destrier (medieval warhorse) was named after the Latin word *dexter* for "on the right." It may have come from the squires' practice of leading horses on their right side. It may also refer to their having been trained to lead with the right leg, allowing them to swerve to that side, away from an opponent on the knight's left.

Longbow Versus Crossbow

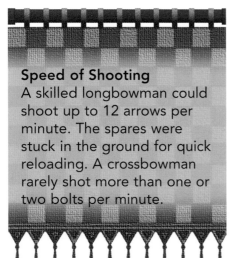
Throughout the medieval period, the longbow and crossbow were the main missile weapons in sieges and on the battlefield, although slings were still sometimes used. The longbow, especially, needed constant practice to draw the string and perfect the aim. The crossbow, whose cord was also at first pulled back by hand, soon became so powerful that mechanical aids were needed. These allowed a much weaker man to use it—he needed only to learn to aim properly.

A long wooden Viking bow has been found, but the powerful form of longbow seems to have been first used in the twelfth century by the south Welsh. By the late thirteenth century, Edward I was gathering large groups of archers, and English and Welsh longbowmen remained a part of the army until Tudor times.

The bow was a single shaped piece of wood—usually yew from Spain or Italy—that made use of the natural springiness. Provided with carved "nocks" for the string at the tips, the bows needed a substantial force—a draw weight of at least 100 to 140 pounds—to be pulled.

A fifteenth-century English archer gets into position behind defensive stakes. At his belt is a small fist shield called a buckler.

The arrows varied. Wide, barbed heads had long cutting edges for hunting but could also be used against horses. The bodkin was a slim, needlelike point that could burst mail rings apart. Later arrows seem to have been reinforced with steel to penetrate plate armor. The effective range was about 110 to 330 yards, when a blizzard of shafts could be sent against an enemy as they approached. Sometimes, archers stood behind a protective screen of sharpened wooden stakes that were cut and carried.

A well-armed archer has stuck his arrows in the ground for quick reloading.

Early crossbows had a wooden bow, spanned by

pressing the feet against the bow and pulling the cord back over a revolving nut released by a trigger. Soon, a more powerful bow of horn and animal sinew was developed, and the steel bow was devised in the fourteenth century. At first, a belt hook was used to pull back the cord of the more powerful crossbows, but mechanical aids were needed for the still stronger bows. These included a lever, a claw that hooked over the cord and was wound back by a ratchet, and a windlass.

A crossbow cord is winched back by a windlass, which used winders often helped by pulleys.

Longbows Triumph
The following account from about 1370 describes an encounter at the Battle of Crécy in 1346, when Genoese crossbowmen fighting for France opposed English and Welsh longbowmen:
"The Genoese hulloa'd a second time and advanced a little farther, but the English still made no move. Then, they raised a third shout, very loud and clear, and began to shoot. At this, the English archers took one pace forward and poured out their arrows on the Genoese so thickly and evenly that they fell like snow."
(From *Chronicles of England*, Jean Froissart)

Cannon and Powder

It is not clear who invented gunpowder. The Chinese had been making fireworks for hundreds of years and had a recipe for producing bombs in the eleventh century. The first recorded pictures of a cannon in Europe appear in two English manuscripts dated 1326–7. In each, the gun barrel, shaped like a vase, lies on a table and fires a large arrow, apparently with brass feathers. It was probably used against enemy soldiers trying to rush out of a castle gate.

Very large guns were laid on solid wooden beds using cranes. They were called bombards, and their purpose was to blast down walls. By the fifteenth century, however, lighter guns were being mounted on wheeled carriages and pulled by horses. Barrels were of two kinds: Bombards and some others were made from long iron strips placed side by side and kept in place by iron hoops slipped over them, as in barrel making; others were cast from bronze.

This bombard, Mons Meg, was built in 1449. It is shown on its modern carriage in Edinburgh Castle, Scotland.

Fifteenth-century Swiss soldiers use field guns, handguns, and pikes.

Cannonballs were at first made from stone, carefully carved into a sphere that fitted the barrel. But by 1500, cast-iron balls were coming into use. Other forms of ammunition were being made: shells that burst into small fragments, containers that flung out a mass of small pieces against soldiers, or star shells that lit up a night sky.

Gunpowder was either ladled with a long handle, or cloth bags were rammed into a barrel, and fine powder was scattered around the touchhole. A hot iron or the glowing tip of a slow match (a piece of oil-soaked cord on a forked staff) was then pressed against this powder to create a spark that flashed through the hole to set off the main charge in the barrel.

Handguns were small guns that fired lead balls, which soldiers could carry. They were in use by the late fourteenth century: at first, as simple cast-iron tubes with either a metal rod or wooden stock to push against the shoulder to take the recoil when fired. The powder was set off by a hot rod or slow match—although by 1500, some had a basic form of trigger. Some were hooked over a wall that absorbed recoil. These became known as "hook guns."

Handguns slowly took over from the longbow and crossbow during the sixteenth century. Handgunners, together with massed ranks of infantry bearing pikes or bills, were common in most European armies, which now fielded similar forces. In Spain, cavalry known as jinets were armed with light javelins. Massed pikemen with handgunners and cannons would remain the mainstay of armies well into the seventeenth century.

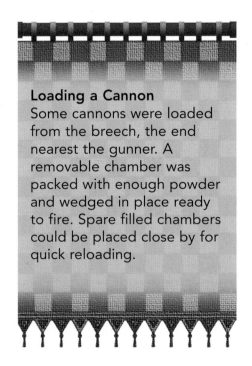

Loading a Cannon
Some cannons were loaded from the breech, the end nearest the gunner. A removable chamber was packed with enough powder and wedged in place ready to fire. Spare filled chambers could be placed close by for quick reloading.

Timeline

1066	Norman invasion of England.
1095	Preaching of the First Crusade.
1099	Capture of Jerusalem by Crusaders.
1187	Crusaders defeated by Saladin at the Horns of Hattin; Saladin captures Jerusalem.
1191	Battle of Arsuf: Richard I holds off Saladin.
1204	Sack of Constantinople by Fourth Crusade and founding of the Latin Empire.
1215	King John seals Magna Carta.
1242	Russians under Alexander Nevsky defeat Teutonic Order at Lake Peipus.
1230–83	The Teutonic Order of German knights conquers and settles in Prussia.
1291	Capture of Acre and loss of Holy Land by Christians.
1297–1305	William Wallace leads Scottish War of Independence.
1298	Battle of Falkirk: Scots pike formations defeated by English under Edward I.
1302	French invading army beaten by Flemish townsmen at Courtrai.
1314	Battle of Bannockburn: English defeated by Scots under Robert the Bruce.
1337	Hundred Years War breaks out between England and France.
1346	Battle of Crécy: French defeated by English under Edward III.
1348–50	The Black Death rages through Europe, killing a third of its people.
1386	Battle of Sempach: Swiss defeat and drive out Austrians.
1410	Battle of Tannenberg: Poles defeat the Teutonic Order.
1415	Battle of Agincourt: French defeated by English under Henry V.
1420–31	The Hussite Wars between the German Empire and Bohemian rebels.

1429	The siege of Orléans by the English is raised by Joan of Arc. Battle of Patay: French defeat English.
1453	Hundred Years War ends, and the English leave France.
1454	Wars of the Roses break out in England between Yorkists and Lancastrians.
1456	Gutenberg produces printing for the first time, in Mainz, Germany.
1461	Battle of Towton: Edward IV defeats Lancastrians in England's bloodiest battle.
1469–92	Lorenzo de' Medici rules in Florence.
1477	Battle of Nancy: Swiss defeat and drive out Burgundians.
1485	Battle of Bosworth: Richard III defeated by Henry Tudor, who establishes the Tudor dynasty in England.
1492	Granada falls and all of Spain comes under the Catholic kings. Columbus lands in America.

The First Knights

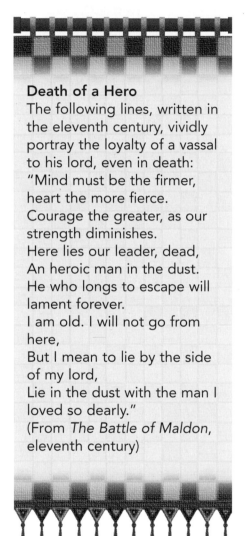

Death of a Hero
The following lines, written in the eleventh century, vividly portray the loyalty of a vassal to his lord, even in death:
"Mind must be the firmer, heart the more fierce.
Courage the greater, as our strength diminishes.
Here lies our leader, dead,
An heroic man in the dust.
He who longs to escape will lament forever.
I am old. I will not go from here,
But I mean to lie by the side of my lord,
Lie in the dust with the man I loved so dearly."
(From *The Battle of Maldon*, eleventh century)

Knighthood grew out of a system known as feudalism, in which a king or lord gave land or property to an individual, his "vassal," in exchange for military service. The vassal swore loyalty to his lord and agreed to fight for him when necessary. In return, he received his lord's protection.

Since the collapse of the Roman empire in the fifth century, Europe had existed in a state of almost continual warfare between rival states. Soldiering was a way of life for most men, and it was a brutal business, with bands of armed men roaming the countryside.

Feudalism, however, valued the virtues of loyalty and service to a leader, and gradually, a new code of military conduct emerged. Instead of just attacking and pillaging at random, men began to see themselves as united in fighting for a purpose. They took pride in putting their military skills at the service of their lord. This attitude was the beginning of knighthood. It soon spread throughout Europe, arriving in England with the Normans when they conquered the country in 1066. Allegiance to a lord was already at the heart of Anglo-Saxon society, and this new, refined concept of knighthood soon took root.

This sixth-century mosaic shows a Vandal, one of the earliest mounted soldiers.

The famous Bayeux Tapestry records how the new cavalry tactics of William of Normandy and his knights surprised the English at the Battle of Hastings.

The Normans built a network of castles throughout England to help them govern each area, and it was in these great households that the tradition of knighthood became established. As well as physical strength and courage, knighthood demanded obedience, endurance, and a serious and careful approach to life—the early knights aimed to embody Christian virtues. Because they all shared the same ideals, knights came to see themselves not just as English or French but as members of a special international brotherhood. Only the son of a knight could become a knight himself.

Although military life remained at the heart of knighthood, there was a peacetime role as well, since the knight served his lord as escort and companion and in general household duties. With the cult of chivalry during the thirteenth and fourteenth centuries, the knight emerged as the romantic figure we think of today.

Charlemagne

Charlemagne, King of the Franks from 768 to 814 and Holy Roman Emperor from 800 to 814, was a great warrior who fought constantly to spread Christianity throughout Europe but who also cared about culture, art, and music. Although he lived 300 years before the medieval period, Charlemagne embodied all the knightly virtues. Many of the epic poems and songs that celebrated his triumphs were revived by medieval knights as inspiration for their own exploits.

Orders of Knighthood

The Order of the Garter
Edward III intended to found an Order of the Round Table, inspired by King Arthur. Ultimately, he formed the Order of the Garter, composed of 25 knights, all of whom had fought with him in the Battle of Crécy in 1346, and 25 priests, who prayed for them in the Order's chapel at Windsor. The Order also paid for the upkeep of 25 poor knights. It gained its name from an incident at court, when a lady lost her garter during a lively dance. The king picked it up and fastened it to his own leg. Everyone was shocked, but the king said, "Evil be to him who evil thinks" ("Honi soit qui mal y pense"), which became the Order's motto.

Edward III awards the Order of the Garter to his son, Edward the Black Prince, who had fought bravely at the Battle of Crécy.

Most knights belonged to an association known as an Order. They swore oaths of loyalty to the Order and its Grand Master, and wore a sash or a badge to identify themselves. The earliest Orders were founded by the Church. The most famous of these were the Knights Templar and the Hospitallers, or Knights of St. John.

Both these Orders were formed during the Crusades, a series of wars between the eleventh and thirteenth centuries in which European Christian armies attempted to conquer the Holy Land, an area of the Middle East ruled by Muslims (see pages 114–115). The Knights Templar were founded to protect Christian pilgrims in the Holy Land, while the Hospitallers cared for sick pilgrims in Jerusalem.

Both Orders became crack fighting forces. "They are milder than lambs and fiercer than lions. They combine the meekness of monks with the fighting courage of knights so completely, that I do not know whether to call them knights or contemplatives." This was how Bernard of Clairvaux described the Knights Templar. The Order had over 20,000 knights and became very rich and powerful.

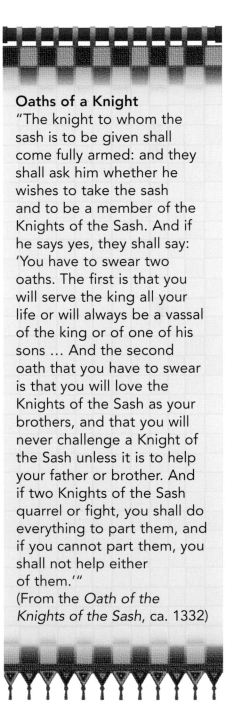

Following the failure of the Crusades, however, knights became disillusioned with the Church's ideals. They turned instead to the old books of romance, especially the tales of King Arthur and his knights. Inspired by these, they began to found new secular Orders.

The new Orders were under the patronage of either the monarch or a noble and were inspired by the ideals of chivalry. Knights were now bound to each other and to their king by oaths of personal loyalty, rather than by religion. This was a good political move. It enabled the king to raise an army more quickly, and he also knew that a knight who had sworn loyalty to him was less likely to rebel against him. These Orders still had a religious connection, however. Each was dedicated to a particular saint and celebrated that saint's feast day.

The secular Orders had rather romantic names and were sometimes dedicated to particular ideals. The Order of the White Lady on a Green Shield, for example, was sworn to protect defenseless ladies. Others included the Order of the Star, the Sash, the Golden Fleece, the Crescent, the Golden Shield, and the Falcon.

Oaths of a Knight
"The knight to whom the sash is to be given shall come fully armed: and they shall ask him whether he wishes to take the sash and to be a member of the Knights of the Sash. And if he says yes, they shall say: 'You have to swear two oaths. The first is that you will serve the king all your life or will always be a vassal of the king or of one of his sons … And the second oath that you have to swear is that you will love the Knights of the Sash as your brothers, and that you will never challenge a Knight of the Sash unless it is to help your father or brother. And if two Knights of the Sash quarrel or fight, you shall do everything to part them, and if you cannot part them, you shall not help either of them.'"
(From the *Oath of the Knights of the Sash*, ca. 1332)

Chivalry

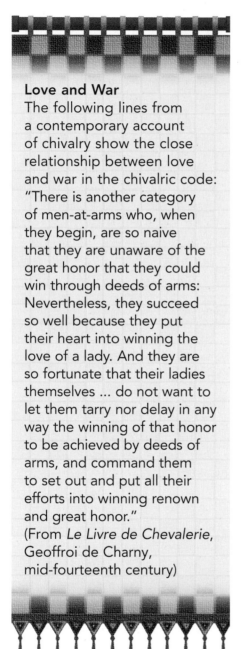

Love and War
The following lines from a contemporary account of chivalry show the close relationship between love and war in the chivalric code:
"There is another category of men-at-arms who, when they begin, are so naive that they are unaware of the great honor that they could win through deeds of arms: Nevertheless, they succeed so well because they put their heart into winning the love of a lady. And they are so fortunate that their ladies themselves ... do not want to let them tarry nor delay in any way the winning of that honor to be achieved by deeds of arms, and command them to set out and put all their efforts into winning renown and great honor."
(From *Le Livre de Chevalerie*, Geoffroi de Charny, mid-fourteenth century)

A knight's lady was sacred because she represented an earthly version of the Virgin Mary, to whom he had dedicated himself.

Chivalry was the code of conduct that transformed the knight from a fighting machine into an idealistic figure. The word itself comes from chevalier, the French word for "knight." It emerged in the twelfth century and declined in the late Middle Ages.

The knight had to dedicate himself to carrying out brave deeds, performed unselfishly and from the noblest of motives. Everything he did was supposed to be based on trust, loyalty, and a generosity of spirit that raised the knight above common men.

One of the most important aspects of chivalry was the protection of women, who were treated almost like saints. Each knight chose a lady to whom he dedicated himself in a relationship called "courtly love." This was not like a real courtship but purely idealistic—often, the lady was already married to someone else, perhaps even to the knight's lord. The knight worshiped her at a distance, hoping for her approval.

Once this had been won, her inspiration gave him courage and strength to succeed in a quest or to win a tournament. The knight also had to defend the lady's honor and write poems praising her beauty and nobility. When he fought in a tournament, he wore a token, such as her handkerchief or glove.

This celebration of chaste and honorable love was the highest ideal of chivalry, but it was also unrealistic. Medieval women were not just passive figures waiting at home in the castle. Many of them were able, wealthy women who managed estates for long periods while their husbands were away on campaigns. They frequently used the men's adoration as a way of encouraging them toward more civilized behavior.

Chivalry also had a place on the battlefield. There were rules about surrender, the honorable treatment of enemies, and the payment of ransoms. Knights were forbidden to bear arms against each other except in warfare. The highest honor for a knight was to have his bravery acknowledged by the enemy, whom he regarded as a brother-in-arms.

Although chivalry encouraged the performance of daring deeds, it disapproved of knights who allowed themselves to be carried away by romantic enthusiasm. In spite of this, many knights lost their lives in foolish escapades, both on the battlefield and in peacetime.

A knight receives a token from his lady before a tournament. The loss of this to his opponent, if he was defeated, was more shaming than defeat itself.

A Knight's Promise
A knight's word of honor was sacred. Froissart, chronicler of the Hundred Years War, tells us that after the Battle of Crécy in 1346, the English army needed safe passage through French territory. A captured French knight, Villiers, was chosen to carry this request to the French king. He was released from prison on his solemn promise to return there when his mission was complete. Villiers was so determined to keep his word that he ignored all the king's attempts to persuade him not to return. The king, in turn, was so impressed by his honesty that he agreed to grant the English safe passage.

Heraldry

Heraldry is the system of visual images by which noble families identify themselves. It began as a means of distinguishing one knight from another in tournaments, when they all wore full armor and helmets which covered their faces.

This Roll of Arms, known as the Herald's Roll, shows the increasing social significance of England's great families in the 1270s.

Heraldic Language
Heraldry has its own language that is still in use today. Many of the words come from French. When describing colors, heralds never mention gold and silver, but "or" and "argent." Similarly, "sable" is black, "gules" red, "vert" green, "azur" blue, and "purpur" purple. They also use unusual terms for everyday images: "Garb" means a wheatsheaf, "manche" is a lady's sleeve, while "lion rampant" means a lion standing on its hind legs, and "lion passant" means a lion walking sideways. The geometric patterns also have names—chief, fess, chevron, bend, and bar—depending on exactly how they appear.

Each knight chose a symbol, or "device," and painted it on his shield on a colored background. Usually, he chose an image that had special significance for his family. If they owned farmland, for example, he might choose a sheaf of wheat. Animals like lions, leopards, and dragons were also popular because they suggested bravery. The knight used this image first on his shield, but it also appeared on the surcoat he wore over his armor, on the harness of his horse, and on the banner he carried. It became his badge of identity.

Heralds were originally the men who arranged and conducted tournaments, and they were the ones responsible for keeping records of these personal devices, or "coats of arms." They compiled Rolls of Arms, listing all the arms of the great families in the land, from the king downward.

These simple images soon became more complex. When families were linked by marriage, their devices were combined. If an eldest son became a knight in his own right, he had to adapt his coat of arms in a way that showed his exact relationship to his father. He might repeat the same images but separate them by a geometric stripe, for example, or use a different background color.

In this way, heraldry became more than a means of identification. It was the visual expression of a knight's status and family pride. It proclaimed his ancestry and his family's noble connections in a way that was easily seen, even by people who could not read.

The simple device that had identified the knight in a tournament became a family badge that appeared on all his household items, on flags, and as a seal on important documents. Very soon, the fact that a man had a coat of arms became the one important thing that established him as a knight.

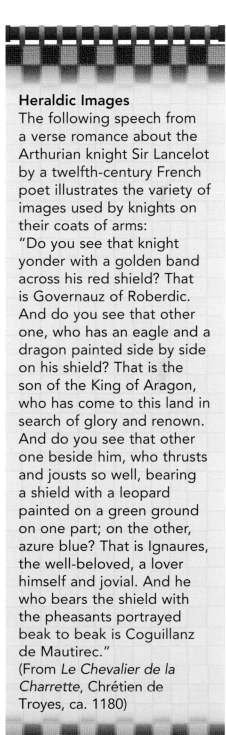

The fifteenth-century Italian knight, Villani of Florence, chose a mythical beast, possibly a griffin, for his coat of arms.

Heraldic Images
The following speech from a verse romance about the Arthurian knight Sir Lancelot by a twelfth-century French poet illustrates the variety of images used by knights on their coats of arms:
"Do you see that knight yonder with a golden band across his red shield? That is Governauz of Roberdic. And do you see that other one, who has an eagle and a dragon painted side by side on his shield? That is the son of the King of Aragon, who has come to this land in search of glory and renown. And do you see that other one beside him, who thrusts and jousts so well, bearing a shield with a leopard painted on a green ground on one part; on the other, azure blue? That is Ignaures, the well-beloved, a lover himself and jovial. And he who bears the shield with the pheasants portrayed beak to beak is Coguillanz de Mautirec."
(From *Le Chevalier de la Charrette*, Chrétien de Troyes, ca. 1180)

A Knight's Training

The Ceremony of Knighting
The following lines describe preparations for the knighting of Geoffrey of Anjou:
"On the great day, as was required by the custom for making knights, baths were prepared ... After having cleansed his body and come from the purification of bathing, [he] dressed in a linen undershirt, putting on a robe woven with gold and a surcoat of a rich purple hue: His stockings were of silk, and on his feet, he wore shoes with little gold lions on them ... He wore a matching hauberk [mail coat] made of double mail ... He was shod in iron shoes, also made from double mail. To his ankles were fastened golden spurs. A shield hung from his neck, on which were golden images of lioncels [lions]. He carried an ash spear and finally a sword from the royal treasure, bearing an ancient inscription."
(From *Chronicles of the Counts of Anjou*, ca.1100–1140)

Before they could face a real opponent, knights had to practice tilting at the quintain.

At first, only the son of a knight could become a knight himself. He began his training early, learning from his father. At the age of seven or eight, he was sent away to the home of another knight, often an uncle or his father's lord, where he began his real apprenticeship. Serving first as a page and then as a valet to his lord, he learned horsemanship and how to fight with sword, shield, and lance. He also learned to look after armor and was taught some elements of military strategy.

When he was about 15, he became a squire, a personal attendant to a particular knight. Here, he probably got his first taste of action, following his lord into battle or to a tournament.

Just as important as military training, however, were civility and good manners. These set the knight apart from the common soldier. As well as learning to read and write, daily life in the great household taught him the social skills of conversation, table manners, and general courtesy. He also had to be good at singing, dancing, writing poetry, and the various games that made up the household's entertainment.

The investiture of a knight was an occasion of great spiritual significance, although the lavish ceremony often overshadowed this.

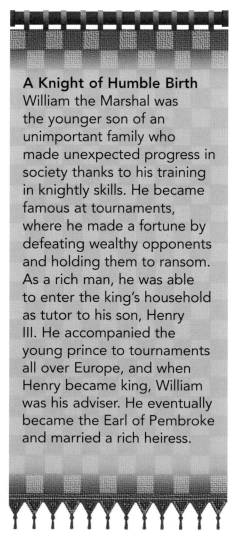

A Knight of Humble Birth
William the Marshal was the younger son of an unimportant family who made unexpected progress in society thanks to his training in knightly skills. He became famous at tournaments, where he made a fortune by defeating wealthy opponents and holding them to ransom. As a rich man, he was able to enter the king's household as tutor to his son, Henry III. He accompanied the young prince to tournaments all over Europe, and when Henry became king, William was his adviser. He eventually became the Earl of Pembroke and married a rich heiress.

Only when he had mastered all these skills, at the age of about 21, was a young man ready to go through the solemn ceremony that would make him a full knight. He spent the night before this ritual praying and fasting, and then he was bathed and dressed in ceremonial clothes. The highlight of the ceremony was when he was touched on the shoulder with the flat blade of a sword and given his full title. This was called "dubbing." This ceremony, the most important of a knight's life, usually took place at court or in the castle, but in times of war, squires were sometimes knighted on the battlefield. This was usually a reward for some particularly brave deed. In this way, a few boys who were not sons of knights but had shown great courage, managed to attain knighthood.

A Knight's Life

A knight was "retained" by a local nobleman. This meant that he was one of the men the nobleman could call on when he himself was required by the king to provide soldiers for a campaign. The usual contract stated that the knight was retained for service "in peace and war, at home and abroad, and in the Holy Land."

In this fifteenth-century painting, a knight pays homage to his lord when he arrives at a military camp.

Hunting Skills

Almost every aspect of a knight's life prepared him for warfare. Hunting was popular not just because it was exciting, but because it was a way of improving horsemanship, keeping men fit, and encouraging them to plan strategies for the chase. All this would be useful to them in their military life. Manuals on hunting were almost as popular as books of chivalry, and all the tales of famous knights include hunting episodes. These usually involved chasing a mysterious animal such as a stag, which led the knight into some strange adventure.

Some knights were bound to their lord as a lifelong commitment, while others were retained on a temporary basis, so that a knight might serve more than one lord in his lifetime. The knight was not paid wages for his service, but he received goods and favors in return. Sir Bartholomew de Enfield, for example, was retained by the Earl of Hereford in 1307 and given hay for four horses, wages for three grooms, and land worth 40 marks [German money] a year. If he went to war or to a tournament, this increased to eight horses and seven grooms.

Battles and fighting were a way of life for many in medieval society, and a knight spent a good deal of his life away on campaigns. There were major foreign wars, such as the Crusades or the Hundred Years War between England and France. In between, there was usually some lesser campaign going on against the Scots or the Welsh. At a local level, too, feuds between rival barons frequently descended into violence. The knight might be called on to serve in any of these campaigns.

Life at home was not very different from warfare. A knight served in the retinue of his lord, accompanying him on pilgrimage or when he was required by the king to appear at ceremonial occasions. Most importantly, he was also retained to fight for his lord in tournaments, which demanded just as much skill as warfare.

A knight might also be awarded the guardianship of a castle on his lord's behalf, where he had hunting rights and other benefits. At home, however, the knight enjoyed the civilizing company of women and had time to read and practice the other arts he had learned as a page.

Women also enjoyed hunting and hawking.

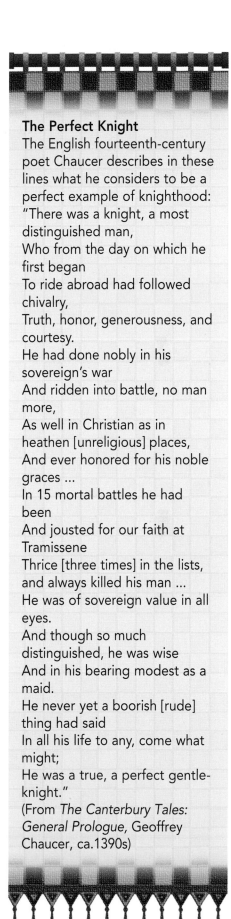

The Perfect Knight
The English fourteenth-century poet Chaucer describes in these lines what he considers to be a perfect example of knighthood:
"There was a knight, a most distinguished man,
Who from the day on which he first began
To ride abroad had followed chivalry,
Truth, honor, generousness, and courtesy.
He had done nobly in his sovereign's war
And ridden into battle, no man more,
As well in Christian as in heathen [unreligious] places,
And ever honored for his noble graces ...
In 15 mortal battles he had been
And jousted for our faith at Tramissene
Thrice [three times] in the lists, and always killed his man ...
He was of sovereign value in all eyes.
And though so much distinguished, he was wise
And in his bearing modest as a maid.
He never yet a boorish [rude] thing had said
In all his life to any, come what might;
He was a true, a perfect gentle-knight."
(From *The Canterbury Tales: General Prologue*, Geoffrey Chaucer, ca.1390s)

A Knight's Armor

Dressing a Knight
The following lines from a poem show how complex the business of getting dressed for battle was in medieval times:
"Then they set the steel shoes on the strong man's feet,
Lapped his legs in steel with lovely greaves [lower leg armor],
Complete with knee pieces, polished bright
And connecting at the knee with gold-knobbed hinges.
Then came the cuisses [thigh armor], which cunningly enclosed
His thighs thick of thew [muscle], and which thongs secured.
Next the hauberk [mail tunic], interlinked with argent steel rings
And resting on rich material, wrapped the warrior around.
He had polished armor on arms and elbows,
Glinting and gay, and gloves of metal,
And all the goodly gear to undergo what might betide.
With richly wrought [decorated] surcoat
And red-gold spurs to ride,
And sword of noble note
At his silken-girdled side."
(From *Sir Gawain and the Green Knight*, II, iv, late fourteenth century)

The design of armor changed considerably during the medieval period to keep pace with new advances in weaponry. In the twelfth century, the knight's body armor was a full-length hauberk, or tunic, made of tiny interlocking rings of metal known as mail, or chain mail. Under this, he wore a linen shirt and breeches. The hauberk had a hood, also of mail, which framed his face like a balaclava when it was pulled up and was lined with fabric for comfort. The metal helmet worn over this was more like a round cap, with a strip coming down to protect the nose, and it was attached to the hauberk by leather laces. Later in the century, hauberks were shortened to thigh length and were worn with leggings, also made of chain mail.

These eleventh-century spurs, intended for everyday use, are very simple. Later, a knight's tournament spurs might be made of engraved gold or silver.

Although chain mail was flexible and allowed the knight to move freely, it was hard to maintain because it rusted and the links broke easily. Also, while it gave some protection against sword strokes, it was easily pierced by arrows.

As the longbow came into use in the thirteenth century, mail gave way to plate armor. At first, knights simply fitted metal plates over their knees and elbows, but eventually, the whole body was encased in metal armor, with a chain mail "ventail" around the neck to cover the vulnerable area between armor and helmet. Over his armor, the knight wore a linen surcoat, on which his coat of arms appeared.

Helmets were by now generally round, either with slits for the eyes or with a visor that could be slid up and down. Attached to the feet were spurs, sharp metal points to help the knight urge on his horse. These new suits of armor gave better protection but could become very hot for the wearer. However, contrary to popular belief, they were not too heavy or cumbersome. A suit of plate armor allowed good flexibility of movement—essential for any knight engaged in battle.

The best armor came from Italy, Germany, and Flanders. By the fifteenth century, armor was sometimes elaborately engraved. Very expensive and highly prized, it was often included in the ransom demanded when a knight was captured.

Spurs

Spurs carried particular symbolic significance in the knight's armory. When he was knighted, especially if this happened on the battlefield as a result of some particularly brave deed, he was said to have "won his spurs." If a knight was disgraced, the spurs were torn from his feet. In the famous Order of the Falcon, special golden spurs were awarded to knights who had been on crusade. One spur meant that he had been on campaign; two meant that he had seen action against the enemy.

Armor changed a great deal over the centuries. The Norman knight of 1066 (left) would hardly recognize the metal-clad fighter of 1480 (right).

| 1066 | 1180 | 1250 | 1340 | 1380 | 1480 |

A Knight and His Weapons

A Knight's Horse

Horses were invaluable, and the knight needed a selection of different breeds. For social riding, hunting, and traveling between battles, he rode a palfrey—a light, swift saddle horse that could also be ridden by ladies. Only the huge warhorse, or destrier, however, could carry a fully armed knight into battle. These were like cart horses, over 6.5 feet high at the withers (shoulders), heavily built, and tiring to ride. The squire rode a strong but less purebred horse known as a rouncy. Like their riders, horses often wore elaborate armor for war or tournaments, with helmets and ornamental breastplates adorned with trinkets and sometimes jewels.

In this painting of the Battle of Auray in 1364, soldiers are fighting with longbows, lances, swords, and axes.

A retained knight had to provide his own weapons. These included a sword and shield, a lance or spear, and a dagger. Tournament weapons were identical to those of real warfare, except that they were lighter and supposed to be blunt, although this rule was not always obeyed.

The wooden lance, iron-tipped and up to 10 feet long, was carried under the knight's arm and later, on a swivel attached to his armor, which made it easier to aim. This was the first weapon of the knight's armory. The sword and shield was the next stage, for closer encounters. Warding off blows with his shield while slicing with his own sword was the knight's greatest skill, either on horseback or on foot.

A squire was responsible for keeping his knight's weapons in good working order, and he also helped arm him for battle.

Once dismounted, he depended on other weapons for close hand-to-hand fighting. These included a type of spiked club called a mace, various types of axes, and a dagger. Many a knight, on foot and clumsy, was killed by a clever dagger stroke between the plates of his armor.

Without a doubt, though, the knight's most essential weapon was his sword. There were many styles, mostly elaborate and with patterns etched into the flat blade. The best were made in Spain. A knight used the same sword throughout his life, and they were often given names. Swords became as famous as the knights themselves. In the old legends, Charlemagne's sword was named Joyeuse and was said to have magical properties, as was King Arthur's sword, Excalibur. Roland, a hero of one of the early chivalric ballads, named his sword Durendal. To keep it from falling into the enemy hands, he tried to destroy it himself.

No knight would dream of using a crossbow or a longbow, which were considered the weapons of the peasant foot soldiers. They were, in any case, impossible to handle on horseback. Nevertheless, they inflicted the most damage in battle. A single arrow from a longbow moved at the speed of a modern rifle bullet and could fell a horse and rider.

Another weapon used against knights was the halberd, a type of spear with an extra curved blade for hooking them off their horses.

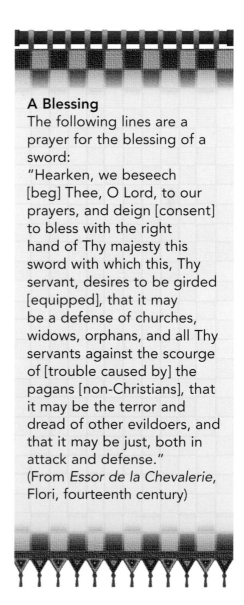

A Blessing
The following lines are a prayer for the blessing of a sword:
"Hearken, we beseech [beg] Thee, O Lord, to our prayers, and deign [consent] to bless with the right hand of Thy majesty this sword with which this, Thy servant, desires to be girded [equipped], that it may be a defense of churches, widows, orphans, and all Thy servants against the scourge of [trouble caused by] the pagans [non-Christians], that it may be the terror and dread of other evildoers, and that it may be just, both in attack and defense."
(From *Essor de la Chevalerie*, Flori, fourteenth century)

111

Knights at War

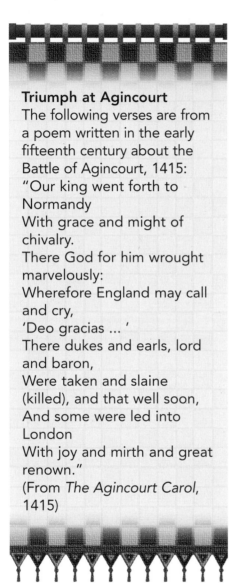

Triumph at Agincourt
The following verses are from a poem written in the early fifteenth century about the Battle of Agincourt, 1415:
"Our king went forth to Normandy
With grace and might of chivalry.
There God for him wrought marvelously:
Wherefore England may call and cry,
'Deo gracias ... '
There dukes and earls, lord and baron,
Were taken and slaine (killed), and that well soon,
And some were led into London
With joy and mirth and great renown."
(From *The Agincourt Carol*, 1415)

In war, a knight might face ranks of others just like himself in mounted combat or—more likely but less exciting—be in command of a battalion besieging a castle or fortified town. Victory usually depended on the capture of such places, and sieges went on for months.

Once the huge catapults had battered the walls, knights were the assault troops who scaled the ladders and stormed the citadel. Guns and gunpowder were hardly known until the fifteenth century, and fighting, when it happened, was mostly on a one-to-one basis. Bands of knights also raided surrounding villages or went in search of supplies, especially if a long siege had exhausted their own food stocks.

Because warfare was so commonplace, people took for granted horrors that we would find shocking today.

Looting of treasure from captured towns was as common in the Hundred Years War as it was in the capture of Jerusalem, shown here.

The siege of Antioch in 1098 lasted for eight months before the city eventually fell to the Crusaders.

A captured town or castle was usually burned, its treasures looted, and innocent civilians cruelly massacred. It was the knight's responsibility to control his troops and prevent the worst of these actions, in accordance with his oaths of charity and chivalry.

If he was involved in individual combat, a knight was more fortunate. Warfare followed the rules of chivalry. For a knight from a good family, being captured was not usually a problem. He could depend on decent treatment at the enemy's hands, and he knew that a ransom would be paid by his family for his release. Although knights pretended to despise these mercenary deals, in reality, ransoms were big business and it was a very common practice.

The adventures of knights in battle were written down by chroniclers. The Battle of Crécy in 1346, for example, was recorded by the French chronicler Froissart, and his account tells us a lot about the period. However, like newspapers today, the chroniclers sometimes made sensational claims about heroic deeds. They also tended to avoid the harsh realities of war.

Every knight dreamed of the glory of dying in battle, but in reality, many died miserably from diseases like dysentery or cholera. King Henry V, victor at Agincourt in 1415, later died like this. Others died from the treatment meant to save them. Some were weakened by bloodletting; others died as a result of excruciating battlefield surgery without anesthetic.

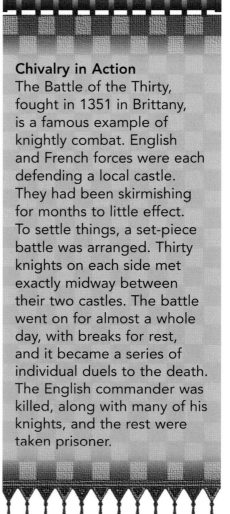

Chivalry in Action
The Battle of the Thirty, fought in 1351 in Brittany, is a famous example of knightly combat. English and French forces were each defending a local castle. They had been skirmishing for months to little effect. To settle things, a set-piece battle was arranged. Thirty knights on each side met exactly midway between their two castles. The battle went on for almost a whole day, with breaks for rest, and it became a series of individual duels to the death. The English commander was killed, along with many of his knights, and the rest were taken prisoner.

The Crusades

For 200 years, the combined Christian armies of Europe tried to drive the Muslim rulers out of the Holy Land and out of the city of Jerusalem in particular. These wars were known as the Crusades.

Jerusalem was sacred to Christians, Muslims, and Jews alike, but at the end of the eleventh century, Christians were being prevented from going there on pilgrimage. This caused outrage in Europe. In 1095, Pope Urban II made a speech calling for a Crusade (known as the First Crusade) to liberate the holy places. On a wave of enthusiasm, thousands of knights set off for the Holy Land, where they succeeded in capturing Jerusalem in 1099. They also established four Crusader states, which they ruled from a chain of castles.

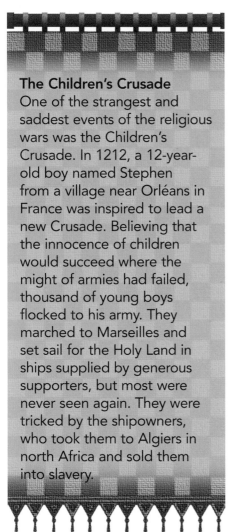

The Children's Crusade
One of the strangest and saddest events of the religious wars was the Children's Crusade. In 1212, a 12-year-old boy named Stephen from a village near Orléans in France was inspired to lead a new Crusade. Believing that the innocence of children would succeed where the might of armies had failed, thousand of young boys flocked to his army. They marched to Marseilles and set sail for the Holy Land in ships supplied by generous supporters, but most were never seen again. They were tricked by the shipowners, who took them to Algiers in north Africa and sold them into slavery.

Outremer ("Overseas") was what the Crusaders called the lands of the Middle East that they conquered. This knight has stayed on there, adopting the dress and customs of the region.

Although the clergy were forbidden to go to war or shed blood themselves, they excused it in the soldiers who went to fight on their behalf. The Pope promised that any knight who died fighting "the infidel" would have all his sins forgiven.

Knighthood became more closely associated with religion, and warfare became not just respectable but honorable. Knights wore red crosses on their tunics as a sign

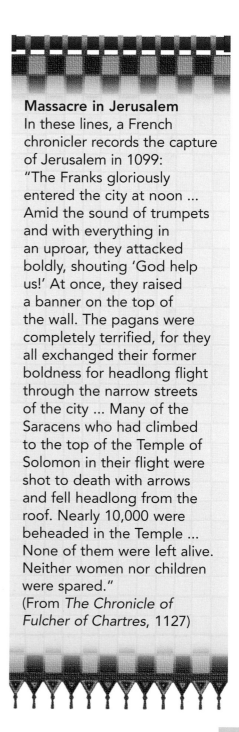

The knight kneeling in prayer here is thought to be King Henry III, who had taken Crusaders vows.

that they had "taken the cross"—the word "crusade" comes from the Latin word crux, meaning "cross." Knights began to see themselves as an international brotherhood united against a common enemy.

Many knights were inspired by genuine religious devotion, but not all crusading was idealistic. There were fortunes to be made in the Holy Land, whether by seizing land, looting treasure, or holding rich enemies to ransom. Many knights returned as wealthy men. Others never returned home but stayed on as rulers of the territory they had captured. They could also behave with great cruelty. When Jerusalem was captured, the Crusaders massacred all the Muslims and Jews in the city, as well as looting its treasures.

Although the First Crusade had been a triumph for the Europeans, Jerusalem was soon recaptured by the Muslims and none of the later Christian armies was so successful. There were eight major Crusades in which thousands of knights died. In the end, however, the great venture was a failure for the Christians, and the Holy Land remained in Muslim hands.

Massacre in Jerusalem
In these lines, a French chronicler records the capture of Jerusalem in 1099:
"The Franks gloriously entered the city at noon ... Amid the sound of trumpets and with everything in an uproar, they attacked boldly, shouting 'God help us!' At once, they raised a banner on the top of the wall. The pagans were completely terrified, for they all exchanged their former boldness for headlong flight through the narrow streets of the city ... Many of the Saracens who had climbed to the top of the Temple of Solomon in their flight were shot to death with arrows and fell headlong from the roof. Nearly 10,000 were beheaded in the Temple ... None of them were left alive. Neither women nor children were spared."
(From *The Chronicle of Fulcher of Chartres*, 1127)

115

Tournaments

Tournaments were the most important events of chivalric knighthood. They were glorious occasions, full of pageantry, and usually lasted several days.

When a tournament was announced, hundreds of knights gathered with their grooms and servants. They pitched their colorful silk tents in the nearby field. Richly dressed ladies watched from a grandstand on the opening day as the knights paraded in full armor, carrying their heraldic banners.

After the pageantry, the serious business of jousting began in the "lists." Two mounted knights armed with lances faced each other across a wooden partition. They charged, each trying to ward off the other's lance with his shield. This went on until one succeeded in knocking the other from his horse and was declared the winner.

Holding the lance steady while controlling an excited galloping charger took all the knight's horsemanship skills.

In some cases, the fighting continued on foot with sword and dagger, until one knight surrendered and had to pay a ransom to gain his freedom. Although they were intended as entertainment, these contests were dangerous occasions and there were many casualties. The tournament ended with a general contest involving all the knights in a ceremonial mock

The Arthurian Tournament
The following extract describes a tournament held by King Arthur at Caerleon: "Every knight in the country who was in any way famed for his bravery wore livery [clothing] and arms showing his own distinctive color, and women of fashion often displayed the same colors. They scorned to give their love to any man who had not proved himself three times in battle. In this way, the womenfolk became chaste and more virtuous, and for their love, the knights were ever more daring ... They went out into the meadows outside the city and split up into groups ... The knights planned an imitation battle and competed together on horseback, while their women watched from the top of the city walls and aroused them to passionate excitement by their flirtatious behavior."
(From *History of the Kings of Britain*, Geoffrey of Monmouth, 1136)

battle. Most of the knights taking part in a tournament appeared as representatives of the lord by whom they were retained. However, because success depended on individual skill, tournaments also attracted a number of wandering knights—"knights errant"—in search of a reputation and the rich prize money on offer.

Fighting was only a part of it, however. In addition to the competing knights and the nobility, tournaments attracted crowds of ordinary folk. Horse dealers, moneylenders, minstrels, and fortune-tellers gave the event the lively air of a carnival. After the combat, knights and ladies spent hours feasting, dancing, playing games, and competing in more sedate sports like archery.

Tournaments were frequently set up around a theme involving costumes and amateur theatricals—"King Arthur and the Round Table" was one popular theme. The craze for tournaments was so great that the nobility tried to outdo each other in staging ever more extravagant displays. Some even went bankrupt in the attempt.

Mock Warfare
The tournament began as a training ground where young men could try out their skills and established knights could practice and keep fit during peacetime. The twelfth-century melee was a free-for-all mock battle, fought over miles of open countryside and involving hundreds of knights on each side. Although the object was to capture and ransom the enemy rather than kill them, many knights were killed or badly wounded. The Church condemned these violent and chaotic episodes. Kings feared them, too, because they were often a cover for the start of a real rebellion.

A costumed tournament joust between a Christian knight and a "Saracen" plays out the Crusades in the safety of England.

Knights of Myth and Legend

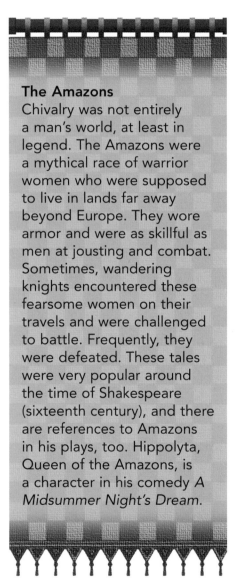

The Amazons
Chivalry was not entirely a man's world, at least in legend. The Amazons were a mythical race of warrior women who were supposed to live in lands far away beyond Europe. They wore armor and were as skillful as men at jousting and combat. Sometimes, wandering knights encountered these fearsome women on their travels and were challenged to battle. Frequently, they were defeated. These tales were very popular around the time of Shakespeare (sixteenth century), and there are references to Amazons in his plays, too. Hippolyta, Queen of the Amazons, is a character in his comedy *A Midsummer Night's Dream*.

St. George's most famous exploit was rescuing a lady from a fearsome dragon.

Knights were always looking to the heroes of the past for inspiration. Charlemagne and Roland, heroes of the earliest ballads, inspired the knights of the twelfth century to rival their glorious deeds. Another popular figure was the Cid, a Spanish knight who rose from humble birth. His loyalty to his king even in the face of wrongful banishment made him an example to all would-be knights.

Because most of these stories were not written down until long after they were supposed to have happened, it is hard to know if they are true and even whether the characters really existed. Saint George, for example, is patron saint of England and of the Order of the Garter. He is often shown killing a dragon. This probably didn't really happen! But George was a real knight, although he actually came from the Middle East and not from England.

In Britain, the most popular stories are those about King Arthur and his Knights of the Round Table. These were already old tales when Sir Thomas Malory wrote them down in the 1400s. Sir Lancelot, Galahad, Gawain, and the other knights experience wonderful adventures in their quest for the Holy Grail, a relic of Christ's crucifixion. Only Galahad, the perfect knight,

Sir Lancelot kneels before King Arthur and Queen Guinevere at the court in Camelot, the starting point for many knightly adventures.

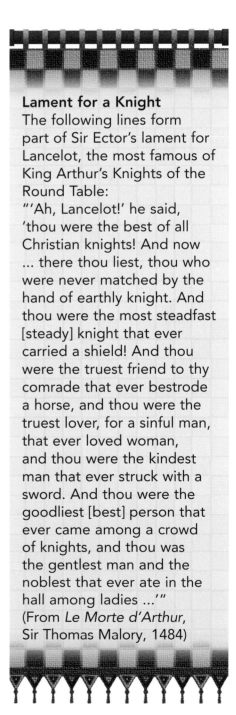

succeeds in the quest, and in the end, the fellowship of the Round Table is destroyed by Lancelot's treachery.

Equally popular in England were tales set during the Crusades. Sir Robert of Loxley, wrongly accused by the wicked Sheriff of Nottingham, becomes the outlaw Robin Hood. Hiding in Sherwood Forest, he continues to perform knightly deeds in secret until King Richard the Lionheart (Richard I) returns. Ivanhoe, created by Scottish novelist Sir Walter Scott in the early nineteenth century, is another knight caught up in the Crusades.

One of the last and most famous of the legendary knights is the Spaniard Don Quixote, an old man inspired by ancient tales to set off on a quest in honor of a beautiful lady. Sadly, he finds that the ideals of chivalry are long dead, and people only make fun of him.

The End of Knighthood

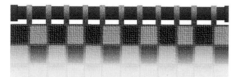

Decline in Chivalric Values
The following extract, from a book written in about 1387, draws a sad contrast between the old ideals of the knight and the new ways of waging war:
"The way of warfare does not follow the ordinances [laws] of worthy chivalry or of the ancient custom of noble warriors who upheld justice, the widow, the orphan, and the poor. And nowadays, it is the opposite that they do everywhere, and the man who does not know how to set a place on fire, to rob churches, and to usurp [seize] the rights and to imprison the priests, is not fit to carry on war. And for these reasons, the knights of today have not the glory and praise of the old champions of former times."
(From *The Tree of Battles*, Honoré Bonet, 1387)

By the end of the fifteenth century, the great tradition of knighthood was in decline. One of the main reasons for this was a change in the army itself. Instead of a brotherhood of noble knights fighting together, the army was now made up of a larger number of professional foot soldiers. These still came from the common people, but they were trained to a higher standard than the old peasant conscripts and needed only a few officers to lead them.

Weapons of war had also changed. Cannons, guns, and gunpowder were now in general use, and shooting from a distance had replaced the knight's style of close-up personal combat.

Foot soldiers and archers face mounted knights in battle during the Hundred Years War.

Another reason for its decline was that knighthood had lost its good reputation in the eyes of ordinary men. People felt that too many men of low birth had been admitted into Orders. There were charges of drunkenness and bad behavior, which fell short of the chivalric ideal. People were disgusted, too, at the way knights had returned from foreign wars with great fortunes, especially since they knew that much of the wealth had come from looted treasure.

Over the years, many unemployed knights had become mercenaries, offering their services to any army for money. Poor or disgraced knights had turned to robbery. Throughout Europe, "free companies" of wandering knights roamed the countryside, fighting the very people they had sworn to protect. Poets of the time had begun to make fun of the ideals of chivalry, instead of glorifying its heroes. All this helped to hasten the end of knighthood.

As knighthood lost its chivalric and military appeal, however, it became more important in the social world. Knights were the third most important social class after the king and the nobility. They made up juries and served in local government. In England, they formed the basis of the House of Commons.

A knighthood was still a great prize, but it was now little more than an honorary title handed out by the king. Knighthood as a way of life to which all young men aspired was gone forever.

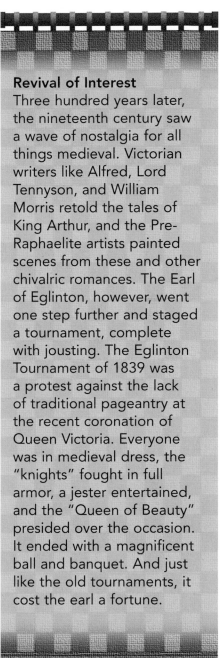

Revival of Interest
Three hundred years later, the nineteenth century saw a wave of nostalgia for all things medieval. Victorian writers like Alfred, Lord Tennyson, and William Morris retold the tales of King Arthur, and the Pre-Raphaelite artists painted scenes from these and other chivalric romances. The Earl of Eglinton, however, went one step further and staged a tournament, complete with jousting. The Eglinton Tournament of 1839 was a protest against the lack of traditional pageantry at the recent coronation of Queen Victoria. Everyone was in medieval dress, the "knights" fought in full armor, a jester entertained, and the "Queen of Beauty" presided over the occasion. It ended with a magnificent ball and banquet. And just like the old tournaments, it cost the earl a fortune.

The artist Edward Burne-Jones made the romantic knightly tales popular all over again in the nineteenth century. This tapestry shows knights setting off on the quest for the Holy Grail.

121

Timeline

500–843   First mounted "knights" appear in Frankish kingdom of France and Germany.

ca. 537   Death of Arthur, King of the Britons.

773–804   Campaigns of Charlemagne and his knights.

1066   England is conquered by the Normans.

1095   Pope Urban II calls for the First Crusade.

1099   Jerusalem captured by knights of the First Crusade.

1120   Foundation of the Knights Templar.

1130   Pope Urban II bans tournaments.

1147–9   The Second Crusade.

1187   Jerusalem recaptured by the Muslim leader Saladin. The Third Crusade.

1190   Order of Teutonic Knights founded in Germany.

1204   Knights of the Fourth Crusade sack Constantinople and set up a Latin Empire.

1212	The Children's Crusade.
1291	Capture of Acre and loss of Holy Land by Christians.
1307–14	Knights Templar investigated for heresy and eventually disbanded.
1307–27	Reign of Edward II, under whom tournaments became lavish occasions.
1337–1453	The Hundred Years War between England and France.
1347	The Order of the Garter founded by Edward III at a tournament at Windsor.
ca. 1350	Guns and other firearms begin to feature in battle.
1415	Battle of Agincourt: French defeated by English under Henry V.
1621	Last official tournament in England.

Glossary

aketon A padded tunic worn under armor or on its own.

allegiance Loyal obedience.

bailiffs Officials employed by town governments.

balaclava A hood that covers the face, with holes for eyes and mouth.

ballad A romantic story told in verse.

ballista A giant crossbow used to shoot at troops during a siege.

barbican A defensive tower built into a castle wall near the gateway.

baron A high-ranking lord who held land from a king in return for service.

basinet A conical or round helmet.

battering rams Heavy beams of wood used for trying to break through castle walls.

bill A farm tool adapted by soldiers for use as a weapon, later made specially for warfare.

bolt A short arrow shot from a crossbow.

borough A large town with its own government and market or fair.

brigandine A coat lined with small plates.

bulwark A defensive wall, often made of earth.

burgage House and shop in a town.

burgess A town dweller who has rights to own property and take part in trade.

catapult A machine used for hurling large rocks at castle walls.

cavalry Soldiers on horseback.

chaplain A religious person in charge of a castle's church.

chattels Small, portable belongings.

cholera A disease caused by dirty water.

citadel Fortress.

clergy Churchmen.

cobbler Maker and mender of shoes.

conscript Someone called for compulsory military service.

contemplative A monk or nun who is dedicated to religious study.

Crusades A series of military expeditions with the aim of breaking Muslim control over what was seen as Christian Holy Land in the Middle East.

cuir-bouilli Leather hardened by soaking or boiling, used to make body armor.

cuisse Plate defense for the thigh.

device Ornamental picture.

dysentery Disease causing diarrhoea.

feud Long-standing rivalry between two people.

feudalism The medieval system by which a vassal held land from a superior in exchange for a service.

flail A spiked bar or ball swung from a long wooden handle.

fool An entertainer who told rude jokes and made fun of important people.

gambeson A padded tunic worn under or over armor.

garrison A body of soldiers ready to fight and defend a castle.

Grail The bowl used by Jesus at the Last Supper.

hauberk A long mail coat.

halberd Staff weapon with an ax-head backed by a hook and topped by a spike, used to pull a knight off his horse.

Holy Land A region of the Middle East, including Jerusalem, held sacred by Christians and Muslims.

homage A ceremonial occasion in the medieval age when a vassal swore loyalty to his ruler and offered his services in return for the land he was given.

infantry Foot soldiers.

infidel Medieval Christians' name for Muslims, literally "those of no faith."

interest fee A fee charged by moneylenders.

jinet A Spanish light horseman.

journeyman A trained craft worker, employed by the day.

jousts Competitions between two knights or men-at-arms who try to knock each other off the horses they are riding.

knight A noble-born medieval soldier on horseback.

lists Barriers enclosing the tournament field.

machicolation The part at the top of a castle wall with holes for dropping stones or hot oil down onto an enemy.

mace A weapon consisting of a heavy metal head attached to a wooden handle.

mail Armor made of interlinked iron rings.

mallets Hammers made out of wood.

mason A person who builds using stone.

master mason The chief mason, in overall charge of the building of a castle.

masterpiece An item of craftwork designed to show the maker's skills and prove that they were good enough to work as a master craftsman.

mayor The leader of town government.

Medieval Age The period of European history between the fall of the Roman Empire in 476 and the fall of Constantinople in 1453.

mercenary A hired soldier.

Middle East The area covered by the land between Egypt and Iran.

migration A movement of people from one country to another country.

minstrel A medieval musician and singer.

nobles Members of a landowning class in Europe in the medieval age.

Normans The descendants of Vikings who settled in northern France and went on to conquer England.

pageantry Ceremonial display.

patronage Favor.

peasants People who worked on a lord's land in return for a small plot of land to grow food for themselves.

philosophy The study of ideas.

pinnacles The very tops of a turrets, shaped like pyramids.

pike A very long spear with a plain head.

pikemen Ordinary soldiers who carried long spears.

pourpoint A padded tunic worn under armor or on its own.

ransom Money paid for the release of a prisoner.

rebellion Fight against one's own lord or king.

Roman Empire The control of Europe and part of the Middle East under the authority of Rome between 31 BCE and 476 CE.

sallet Type of helmet extending backward at the neck.

Saracen A Muslim or any Arab.

secular Not based on religion.

siege An attack on a castle, by surrounding it and preventing supplies and reinforcements from reaching it in the expectation that it will eventually surrender.

skirmish Brief military fight.

smith A worker in metal.

tallow Sheep fat.

tallow candles Candles made from animal fat.

tanning Soaking, cleaning, and scraping the hair off hides, then treating them with mixtures of chemicals to turn them into leather.

theology The study of religion.

tinker A mender of metal pots and pans.

tournament A medieval entertainment that involves jousting.

trencher A slice of stale bread used as a disposable plate.

troubadour A singer or poet of the medieval age.

turret A small tower on a castle wall.

valet Manservant.

vassal A loyal subject or holder of land on the condition of offering a service in return for the land.

visor Hinged flap of helmet that covers the eyes.

warren keeper A rabbit keeper.

Index

Note: Page numbers in bold refer to information contained in captions.